MAKING ROOM FOR Life

Trading Chaotic Lifestyles
for Connected Relationships

RANDY FRAZEE

ZONDERVAN

GRAND RAPIDS, MICHIGAN 49530

We want to hear from you. Please send your comments about this book to us in care of zreview@zondervan.com. Thank you.

ZONDERVAN™

Making Room for Life
Copyright © 2003 by Randy Frazee

This title is also available as a Zondervan audio product. Visit www.zondervan.com/audiopages for more information.

Requests for information should be addressed to:
Zondervan, *Grand Rapids, Michigan 49530*

Library of Congress Cataloging-in-Publication Data

Frazee, Randy.
    Making room for life : trading chaotic lifestyles for connected relationships / Randy Frazee.—1st ed.
      p. cm.
    Includes bibliographical references.
     ISBN 0-310-25016-1
     1. Christian life.   2. Family—Religious life.   I. Title.
    BV4526.3.F73 2004
    284.4—dc22
                                    2003017825

This edition printed on acid-free paper.

Interior design by Beth Shagene

Printed in the United States of America

---

03 04 05 06 07 08 09 /❖ DC/ 10 9 8 7 6 5 4 3 2 1

Praise for *Making Room for Life*

I read *Making Room for Life* sandwiched in the middle seat of a crowded airplane. By the time I finished part 2 ("The Solution: Restructuring Our Relationships and Time"), I noticed that my breathing patterns had become deeper and more relaxed. *Making Room for Life* is the "Mirror of Erised" for life and community. For all those "Harried Potters" out there—take heed.

JOSEPH R. MYERS,
author of *The Search to Belong:
Rethinking Intimacy, Community,
and Small Groups*

Randy Frazee's *Making Room for Life* is the right book at the right time for a frazzled, frantic, and unfulfilled populace. It is a book of sound practical advice from a wise pastor who knows people's needs. The author urges readers to join a small group of fellow seekers, in which lives can be shared at a deep level and the life-transforming discovery made that God is nearer and dearer to us than we can possibly imagine.

GEORGE GALLUP JR.,
chairman, The George H Gallup
International Institute

I'm so excited you picked up this book. In a time when our hectic daily schedules often squeeze the living out of life, *Making Room for Life* is a godsend. Connection and community are essential to healthy living—not just for us, but for our kids as well. Randy Frazee offers a vision of a life rich in relationships and meaning. Best of all, he provides clear steps for making this vision a reality. Life is a precious gift, so make room for it!

KEN BLANCHARD,
coauthor of *The One Minute
Manager®* and *Servant Leader*

"I want to simplify my life, but simplifying is way too complicated!" If that's how you feel, you need to read *Making Room for Life*. If you feel our modern Western pace of living is inhospitable to human life, if you're fed up with what Randy Frazee calls "the severe fragmentation and discontinuity of the American lifestyle," if you have a sneaking suspicion that modern "conveniences" are giving you more time to enjoy life less, then cancel an appointment immediately and let Randy help you discover life without breathlessness.

BRIAN MCLAREN,
pastor (crcc.org),
author, fellow in emergent
(emergentvillage.com)

This practical book is a timely word for a complex culture. Randy's concept of reorganizing our time in a way that flows with creation is powerful and challenging. I highly recommend that you read this work, if you have the time! That's the point!

DAVID A. ANDERSON, D.Phil.,
pastor, Bridgeway Community Church

Imagine if we actually *did* what Randy suggests. [Sigh] It's doubtful we will—but it would be revolutionary!

MARK OESTREICHER,
president, Youth Specialties;
publisher, emergentYS resources
for emerging church leaders

Randy Frazee has made a significant contribution to one of the most important conversations among thoughtful Christians today: "How do we live lives in harmony with God in the context of our world?"

DOUG PAGITT,
pastor, Solomon's Porch

To Rozanne,
my wife and best friend:
my personal journey to make room
for life has been driven by a passion
to spend more time with you

Contents

Part 4: The How-To's: Practical Steps to Making Room for Life

Acknowledgments

Making Room for Life has been a great joy to write. But it has been more than a writing project. It has become a way of life for my family and me. The principal result of this vision is connected relationships—with God and with others. So I want to thank my God for connecting with me through Jesus Christ thirty years ago. I also want to thank God for the many significant people he has brought into my life to encourage me and stand by me.

To my wife, Rozanne, I dedicate this book. To my four children—Jennifer, David, Stephen, and Austin—I thank God daily that he has put you in the room with me. We have experienced such a rich life together. I pray for many more years together. I can't forget my connection with my wife's parents, Al and Joan Bitonti, and my mother and father, Ruth Ann and Ralph Frazee, as well as with our siblings and their families—Don, Teresa, Jo Ann, Mike, Suzanne, and Joi.

So much of what I have learned about making room for life has been learned with the precious families who live in my neighborhood and a little ways down the street— the Ballows, Huffmans, Wellses, Hortons, Lawrences, Sanderses, McNultys, Sparkses, Zangs, Hollandsworths, Vossens, and Wades. May our tribe increase and our relationships deepen even more.

To the current elders of Pantego Bible Church—Jerry McCullough, Ryall Tune, Ed Frazier, Wayne Bailey, George

Lynch, Gregg Williams, Mike Phifer, Steve Newby, and Larry Ivey—you have stood up for me and believed in this vision. Thank you. To the entire staff at Pantego Bible Church—you are the ones who carry the vision to so many others; your tenacity, vision, and work ethic inspire me. To my senior leadership team—Kevin Walker, Pam Forbes, Ira Orr, Scott Burks, and Tom Bulick—thank you for sharing this exciting vision with me, along with helping to carry the burden of making it happen in the lives of the people God has given us to shepherd. And, of course, to the congregation of Pantego Bible Church—your innovative spirit has made our journey possible.

There are certain people who have supported me over the years that I must mention every time I'm able to accomplish something like this. Without them, I just would not have the strength—the Reillys, the Veigels, the Guions, the Joneses, the Hilliards, the Ashtons, and the Wrights. To my mentors and heroes—Bob Buford, Howard Hendricks, George Gallup Jr., Dallas Willard, Larry Crabb, George Barna—I've learned so much from all of you.

Making Room for Life is a book that has enlisted many people to help make it a reality. Rozanne, my wife, was my faithful reader and editor before the manuscript went to Zondervan. The best thoughts in the book are hers. I just take credit for them. This is book number three that Rita Ballow has typed and cared for like a mother hen. I deeply appreciate your faithfulness to help me over the last fifteen years, Rita. To Maria Nutt, my personal assistant: may God continue to give you grace, mercy, wisdom, and strength as you try to manage my life and ministry. It is an impossible job, but somehow you manage to pull it off.

To all of the folks at Zondervan—Jack Kuhatschek, John Raymond, Alicia Mey, Jamie Hinojosa, Jason Pranger, Dirk Buursma, Scott Bolinder, Lyn Cryderman, Stan Gundry—thank you for believing in me once again and for giving me this awesome opportunity to share the "making room for life" vision with others.

Introduction

If you are reading these words, there's a good chance you have some interest in "making room for life." What a concept. A book about the most basic aspect of living—LIFE! As crazy as it may sound, most people I know are ready for it.

What comes to your mind when you see the words "making room for life"? I'll tell you what it means to me, and you tell me whether we're on the same page.

- I envision a life that is not as hectic. We always seem to be on our way to the next place, never really arriving at a destination.
- I envision a life with either more money or less expenses. (I strongly suspect it's less expenses.)
- I envision a life with less time in the car and more time for walks. Can this ever become a reality?
- I envision a life where there is a time for work and a time for play. I love to work, but I just want it to keep from getting offside. I want to play more, but I think after all these years I've forgotten how.
- I envision a life with less fast food in the car and more spreads of home cooking with family and friends. Shoving burritos in our mouths while driving can't be what God had in mind for us. We have lost the beautiful art of sharing a meal together. I want to regain that art.
- I envision a life of less accumulation and more conversation. I already have way too many manuals on how to care for the stuff I bought. Plus, people

have to be more interesting than things. I don't think most of us really know for sure.

My list goes on and on, and I'm sure yours does, too. We are an advanced people with vast resources. We've invented speed and time-saving technology that couldn't be fathomed a hundred years ago. We have more discretionary money than any people in history, though we usually spend it all before it even comes in. We have the freedom to choose like no other people in any other time. With all this going for us, why does it feel as though we've gone backward instead of forward in our quest for a quality life? And how can we do something about it? That's the purpose of this book. It is for those who say, "That's enough!" "I've had it!" "Things are going to be different!"

If this describes you, then you're going to enjoy the pages that follow. We'll start off by unveiling the problem. What causes such a sophisticated people to squeeze living out of life? Once the problem has been diagnosed, we'll move quickly to solutions. How can we restructure our relationships and our time so that we can get at the heart of living? We'll then turn our attention to overcoming the obstacles that threaten our success. We'll wrap up with five practical chapters on the how-to's of making this vision a reality in our lives.

At the end of each chapter you'll be asked to write out your thoughts about what you've read and then to identify one or more action steps to consider as you tailor your own adventure in making room for life. This is important for two reasons. First, this is a journey that begins with baby steps. Don't be discouraged by this. Each step you choose to take will reap great rewards. The baby steps will build momentum and courage for the steps ahead. Second, the ideas presented here are not an "all or nothing" proposition. There may be things that you don't like or that don't make sense for you, given your circumstances. Take what makes sense, and leave the rest alone.

My heart is pounding with excitement as I envision you reading what follows. This has been an exciting and rich experience for my family and me over the last ten years. We are closer than ever to the vision described above. While your list may look a bit different, I have a passion to see you make progress. If you get a chance, let me know your thoughts (e-mail me at response@makingroomforlife.com).

THE PROBLEM:
Squeezing Living
Out of Life

Simply put, many of us have squeezed living out of life. We don't have the time to soak in life and deep friendships. We're always running around trying to get to the next event. This presents at least two major problems. First, our busy lifestyles stimulate a toxic disease called *crowded loneliness*. But there's an even deeper problem. In our original design we were created with a *connection requirement*. If this requirement is not met, we will die.

CHAPTER 1

Crowded Loneliness

Managing Too Many Worlds

Consider the average day of a typical middle-class family in America. The family rises at 6:00 A.M. Everyone fends for himself or herself for breakfast. Dad heads out at 6:45 to beat the 7:00 traffic. His normal commute without excessive traffic is forty-five minutes. Mom and the two children are out the door by 7:15 (usually someone is a little cranky). Mom drops her elementary-age sons off at school by 7:40. Twenty minutes later she arrives at her workplace.

At 3:30 P.M. the children are done with school and enter an after-school program. Mom skips lunch so she can rush out of the office to pick the kids up by 5:00. She arrives home at 5:30. Fifteen minutes later one son has baseball practice. She gets both kids in the car and rushes to make it to the practice field on time. The other son has a game at 8:00. She calls her husband on the cell phone while taking her son to baseball practice to make sure he can grab the second child at the field and get him to his game by 7:30.

Dad leaves the office at 6:00 P.M., unsuccessful in his efforts to make it through his to-do list. Traffic is now an issue. The forty-five-minute commute stretches now into an hour and fifteen minutes. He arrives at the practice field at 7:15 with all the signs of road stress. He kisses his wife, waves to his son in center field, whooshes the second son into his SUV (a mere $700 a month), and heads to the game field about fifteen minutes away. Son #1 finishes practice at 7:30, and he and Mom head for home. On the way they stop at Taco Bell for dinner. They arrive home at 8:00. The boy turns to the video games while Mom checks the e-mail.

Meantime, the baseball game gets started a little late and doesn't end until 9:45 P.M. Dad is still in his business casual clothes, but he does appreciate the forced break to watch his son play ball. On their way home they make a quick stop at the McDonald's drive-in window. They arrive home at 10:30. Once in the house, son #2 reveals that he hasn't finished studying for the history test he's supposed to take tomorrow.

After forty-five minutes of shoving facts into her son's short-term memory while he inhales a McDonald's "Happy" Meal, Mom sends him to bed. It is now 11:15 P.M. Time for bed. Mom and Dad flop into bed dead tired. They watch a little television; exchange a few words—mostly action items for the next day—and then lights go out. Mom falls asleep as soon as the lights are out. Dad, on the other hand, doesn't. He lies there thinking about all the things that must be done. He knows he needs to sleep, so he gets up and swallows a sleeping pill. It seems to be the only way he can get a good night's sleep lately. It bothers him a little, but he doesn't see any alternative. Tomorrow promises more of the same. Things seem a little harried and out of hand, but the following assumptions keep the family from making any changes:

- Everyone lives this way.

- This is a privileged life that can only be maintained with hard work and discretionary money.
- Things will even out soon. This is just a temporary season of busyness.

Maybe this mirrors your life. The activities may be different, but the movement and noise are the same. The initial thought is that the more financial resources you have, the more likely you are to have a stress-free, relaxing life. In reality, though, studies show that with increased resources comes increased complexity, not simplicity. If they aren't especially careful, the ones who have more actually have more with which to destroy themselves.

Maybe you can relate to the cartoon caption below. Can you think of how many times you've made a resolution to do something about busyness and stress in your life only to find nothing really

"Fred, you must learn to relax."

changing? Noise and movement make up so much of our lives that we don't know how to effectively stop when a little "R and R" is attempted. There is among Americans a common illness called "leisure sickness."[1] This malady manifests itself in several forms, such as flulike symptoms, headache, sore throat, and muscle aches. Essentially, our bodies and emotions are so stressed out during the week that in the evenings and particularly the weekends we fall apart. The only prescription for this social fever is a change in lifestyle.

I am the pastor of a large church in a busy suburb, a husband, and the father of four children. The opportunities to send myself into the "rubber room" of insanity abound. Preparing sermons, managing staff, meeting parishioners' expectations, tending to constant changes that need to be implemented, spending time with family, paying individual attention to each of my children, having individual time with my wife, exercising, staying in touch with my extended family, helping with science projects, going to children's sports events—the list goes on and on. I don't know how many times people have approached me with the words "I'm concerned about you; you have too much to handle." I think I lived so long under extreme stress that I lost sense of what was happening. It had become routine and normal. This is a scary place to be.

So the impetus for my initial search for connectedness or community was not a need to prepare a sermon or write a book but a need for personal sanity. I knew I couldn't obtain connectedness by increasing my speed or extending my hours of work. King Solomon tried it about three thousand years ago and found out that it doesn't work. I'm nowhere close to being the smartest guy in the world, but I'm smart enough to listen to the world's wisest person.

I needed something fresh, something deeper. I also had a sense of urgency. Several years ago as my daughter approached her sixteenth birthday, I realized that I wouldn't have much more time with my children, and I didn't think my health would hold out under the daily pressure I was voluntarily inflicting on it. At the same time

I didn't want my life to be meaningless. I didn't want to retire from life and sit on the back-porch rocker watching little birds suck juice out of a jar. I've always lived with a strong sense that God has a calling on my life, that he has something for me to accomplish. But I needed to find some balance and establish some boundaries. Certainly, a big part of what God has for my life is what I can *become* as a person in Christ—not just what I *do* for Christ.

The solutions to my dilemma were rooted in God's Word, coupled with the common sense of sages who have gone before us. It has rescued me from a life of running on a hamster's wheel, a life of motion without meaning.

Managing Your Relationships

Let's begin our journey together with some self-discovery. Grab a pen or pencil and a piece of paper. Now look at the following illustration.

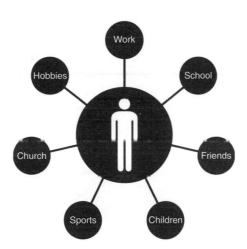

The individual in the center represents a person who is trying to make more room for life. Each of the smaller circles represents a relationship that they manage. They may invest time daily in a particular relationship, or only a few times a year. Think about your life and the various relationships you manage, and draw a circle for each.

When you've completed this, go back to each circle you have drawn and ask yourself the question, "Is that really one relationship group, or are there more worlds within each circle that are managed separately?" For example, if you have more than one child, do they go to the same school? If not, then you need to draw a separate circle for each school. If you are married, does your spouse work? If you don't both work at the same place, then you need to draw an additional circle representing this separate relationship. If you have children, are they involved in sports? If so, are they involved in multiple sports like soccer, baseball, and volleyball? What about music lessons? How about extended family? You should already have a circle representing your family and another circle representing your spouse's family. Do they all live in the same town, or are they spread throughout different states? If they are in different cities or states, then you need to draw a circle for each one. Are you in a blended family situation? If there is joint custody, then you need to draw a circle for each relationship. How about your hobbies? Maybe you have a group you golf with and a group you play cards with. Draw a different circle if these are not the same people. What about past friends you try to maintain contact with—college friends, friends you had in other places you lived, and so forth?

If you live in suburban America, you're probably getting a little stressed by now, but please continue on for a few more minutes. Now consider church. If you are involved in a church, is it really one circle, or are there many circles of different activities and relationships (missions committee, women's groups, choir, youth groups, small group, support group, elder board, and the like)? The average suburban American who is really involved in church life can have four to six different circles. If an entire family is fully involved, there can be as many as fifteen different circles. Draw a circle for each activity or ministry you are involved with. Before you've finished drawing your circles, get some feedback from others about ones you may have overlooked. Be sure you have a circle representing the persons you will ask before you seek their counsel.

Next, you need to consider the line drawn to each circle. These lines represent your commute to these relationships. You may consider drawing an object next to each line that represents the means by which you engage in this relationship. These may be automobiles, airplanes, letters, e-mail, telephones, and so forth. Place a time value on each line representing a round-trip commute to and from that circle. For example, if it takes you an average of forty-five minutes to get to work, write down ninety minutes. I'd invite you to multiply this for the entire month, but it just might put you over the edge.

Now let's consider the issue of commuting in an automobile. Harvard University's Robert Putnam, in his best-selling book, *Bowling Alone,* gives some startling statistics on American commuting.[2] His studies show that the average American family engages in thirteen automobile commutes a day! When I first heard this statistic, I immediately dismissed it as not a reality for my family. However, after taking a moment to calculate the average business and school day, I found myself easily within these parameters. To add to the misery, recent studies suggest that 80 percent of cars on the road systems in cities and suburbs in America only have one person in them—the driver.[3] The only source for two-way interaction is either the unwholesome hand gestures exchanged when one is cut off or the cell phone.

Robert Putnam suggests this formula: For every ten minutes you spend in an automobile, you reduce your available social capital [time for relationships] by 10 percent.[4] If his calculations are accurate, as you look at the drawing of your social world you may conclude that you not only don't have any social capital available at the end of the day, but also that you are going into social debt. If you believe that we are created as social beings who require a quantity (and a quality) of people interaction each day to survive, then this means we are dying—not from physical illnesses only but from social illness as well. I'm quite confident that, as historians look back on this era in which we live, one of the marks we will bear is *the death of community.*

Many people turn to the church to solve their problem of loneliness and disconnectedness. Because the church has been commissioned by Christ to reach out and to develop a functioning community, it is an appropriate place to turn. The church's principal solution for community over the last thirty to forty years has been the small group. Without question, the small group movement has made its mark on society. Studies show that 40 percent of Americans are involved in some kind of small group.[5] Many people get involved in such a group to find a point of connection and a greater sense of intimacy and belonging, to have a place where they can share their fears and dreams. Testimony reveals that small groups are good and helpful. But studies also show that they often don't work.[6]

Thinking of the old Chinese proverb that says "the beginning of wisdom is to call something by its right name," go back to your personal galaxy and add a circle for your small group (if you haven't already). Now rename the small group according to what you see and feel. How about the name "Another World to Manage"? The fault does not lie with the concept of smallness or with the people. The problem lies with *orbit management.* Most people confess to rushing from one world to a totally separate world of small group. In other words, the people in their small group are not involved in any other world they are managing. Very few small group members get together outside of the formal meeting date, not because there isn't a desire, but because there just isn't any time. While attempts are made, there is little chance the members of the small group can get their arms around your world or your arms around theirs. Their lives simply do not intersect anywhere except the small group meeting—and perhaps a quick "hello" at church on Sunday morning. We are simply not principal characters in each other's worlds.

If you haven't done so already, finish drawing your worlds, or add new ones that came to mind as you read. What are your thoughts about what you have drawn? If you're the average person, you'll be seeing a picture of stress. Take some time to give the right name to your life. How about "Lost in Space," or "Everybody Knows My Name, but Nobody Knows Me," or "Planet Hopper," or "Space Shuttle Dweller." How about a new name for your car such as "Cocoon on Wheels" or "Mobile Penitentiary Cell." If we are going to make room for life, these are the kinds of honest confrontations on our existing lifestyles we must have.

As you read the following pages, determine now that you're going to establish your own specific thoughts at the end of each chapter as well as a list of action steps that will move you further from *mere existence* and closer to *authentic living*. My goal and passion are not just to see you exist in a life of crowded loneliness but to give you a vision for a new way of life—along with the practical steps to get there. The ideas will be easy to understand, but the implementation will take courage. But if you're like me and so many others I know, you're ready for a change.

My Thoughts on This Chapter

Small Group Discussion

❏ When you hear the words "making room for life," what does it mean to you? If you successfully made more room for life, what would you be doing?

❏ Share the drawings of your worlds with each other.

❏ Who in your group has the most relationships to manage? Who has the fewest? Why?

❏ How many people in your small group know the people in your other circles?

❏ If the members of your discussion group went with you to visit an individual or group of people from another circle whom they didn't know, what would you want your small group members to know ahead of time? Do you behave differently when you are in different circles (i.e. more talkative, less talkative, leader, follower, respected, not respected, looked up to, looked down on, angry, happy, relaxed, uptight, proud, embarrassed, and so on)?

❏ Share the amount of time you and your family spend in an automobile on an average day or week. Are you satisfied or dissatisfied with the amount of time you spend commuting to your different worlds?

❏ Discuss the difference between "loneliness" and "crowded loneliness." Which of these do you have a tendency to struggle with more?

❏ Share your number one discovery from this chapter.

❏ Identify and share one personal action step you will take to begin making more room for life.

❑ Community-Building Exercise: Go to your local mall as a group. Observe how many people are there but how little interaction is taking place. Count the number of people who are alone. Then treat yourself to a coffee, soda, or a dip of ice cream.

Personal Action Steps

CHAPTER 2

The Connection Requirement

Created for Community

If we hope to be successful in truly making room for life, we're going to have to rebuild our current lifestyles on a new foundation. We cannot simply pour more money and energy into the paradigm of crowded loneliness. Managing an endless number of disconnected linear relationships is exhausting. But more than just making us tired, this way of life is toxic. We were created with a connection requirement, and if this requirement is not satisfied, we will eventually die. If we ever became convinced of this, it would make our pursuit of a connecting life a higher priority. This, then, is the goal of this chapter.

"We" versus "Me"

North Americans have a reverence for individuality and consumerism. It flows from the teaching of men like René Descartes, who popularized the phrase "I think, therefore I am." At first this seems like a rather benign and esoteric philosophic phrase. Its most basic meaning suggests that one's identity flows from oneself. After all, Whitney Houston sang that to love oneself was "the greatest love of all." Without boundaries, Americans have taken the concept of self-identity to a new level afforded them by wealth. In America, success is defined by the next purchase. In other places around the world success is defined by a simple meal and conversation with family and friends. The accumulation of stuff is added to our "net worth" statement that deems us "worthy" in relationship to others who have less. Therefore, we passionately pursue the next purchase in an attempt to raise our perceived value. These are two very different foundations to build a life on with two very different results. We now live by the phrase "I purchase/accumulate, therefore I am."

In one of their "Strange but True" columns titled "Selling the 'me' versus 'we,'" brothers Rich and Bill Sones answered this question: "How are ads that target consumers in individualistic societies such as the United States and Canada different from ads in communal societies such as Korea?"

> The former try to sell EGO and what the product can do for you, the latter sell SOCIAL CONNECTEDNESS and how the product can foster feelings of belonging and harmony. . . .
>
> "Be all that you can be. Join the Army," is a classic U.S. pitch at individualistic ego-enhancement. Toyota's "I love what it does for me. From any angle" (the car pictured front and sideways) succeeds in the U.S., but "The best relationships are lasting ones . . . Toyota Quality" works better in communal Korea. When researchers Sang-Pil Han and Sharon Shavitt tested chewing gum ads in both cultures, they found "Treat yourself to a breath-freshening experience" worked in one but not the other; the same for "Share a breath-freshening experience." Can you guess which was which?[7]

If you, like most people I know, are worn out from a lifestyle of accumulation, then an invitation to a lifestyle of conversation and community is welcome. Our universal longing for community is a validation in and of itself of the connection requirement. It should make us want to run to this new place.

South African Anglican minister the Reverend Desmond Tutu has coined a term that exposes a richer foundation for living—one built on community and conversation in contrast to individualism and accumulation. The term is *ubuntu*. *Ubuntu* is African for "people" and has come to represent a community theology that can be expressed in the phrase "we are, therefore I am." This powerful phrase suggests that one's identity is formed by community.[8] One of the fundamental beliefs of *ubuntu* can be expressed in the African saying *motho ke motho ba batho ba bangwe/umuntu ngumuntu ngabantu*, which means, "A person can only be a person through others."[9] In other words, our perceived value goes up in proportion to our investment in community. This teaching implies that we were designed with a connection requirement. I'd like to further suggest that this belief structure is more in keeping with what God had in mind when he created us.

Created for Connection

How were we made? What are the requirements for us to live a healthy and fruitful life? Let's draw our attention to the original design of human life in Genesis 1–2 to find the answers. In the six-day description of the creation of the heavens and the earth and all living things within it, God makes a journal entry into his construction log: "It is good." This should not surprise us given the scope and depth of God's capacity. On the sixth day, God unveils his supreme creation—us! With the inclusion of the human being into the equation God makes this final comment in chapter 1: "God saw all that he had made, and it was very good." Trinity Construction engaged in history's ultimate design-build project. I'd love to see the drawings on how one goes about setting the sun, moon, and stars in their proper places.

When we get to chapter 2 of Genesis, the author goes into greater detail on God's design and purpose for man. We are told that God took dust from the ground and formed it into the human shape. Then, he breathed into Adam's lifeless nostrils the "breath of life," and Adam became a living being (Genesis 2:7). We are told that God provided a dwelling place for Adam called the Garden of Eden (Genesis 2:8–14). As you read the description of this place you get the idea that Adam had a home that makes Bill Gates's estate look like a tool shed. We are told that Adam was given the job of caring for the garden—which couldn't have been too hard since weeds hadn't yet been created (Genesis 3:18). We're also told that Adam was to eat to his heart's content from any of the trees except one—the tree of the knowledge of good and evil (Genesis 2:16–17). What a deal to have only one law to obey. It would never be this simple again.

Then in Genesis 2:18 the unexpected happens. After six consecutive entries of how good things were—the last entry even suggesting that the whole project was very good—we are not expecting God to say that something is not good, but he does. "The LORD God said, 'It is *not good* for the man to be alone'" (Genesis 2:18, emphasis added). What does this mean?

If God knew that man could not handle human isolation, why did he not deal with this up front on day six? I believe this is God's way of highlighting for us man's need for community. If God had created Eve on the sixth day, along with Adam, we might have taken for granted the absolute importance of companionship and conversation. I think God delayed the creation of Eve to drive the point home that humans have not been created to be alone. In other words, *community is the only change order in creation.* God is saying that he designed humans to require oxygen to live. By the same token, he is also saying that we must have community to live! We are built with a connection requirement.

"We Theology"

For most of my Christian life, I've read the New Testament letters as though the authors were writing to individuals about growing as individuals in Christ. I took the perspective of American individualism and consumerism and read it into Scripture: "Everything is all about me." After gaining an understanding that the mission of the church is to build up and bring to maturity the body of Christ, which is made up of all of us, not just me, I now see that I had been missing the communal purpose of life.

I have a call as an individual to become like Christ in the way I live. This call is empowered by the Spirit of God within me as I yield my life in obedience to God's Word. However, this call must not be seen in isolation, apart from my interaction with other believers. To do so would be like exercising your right arm when you lifted weights but not your left. If you did this over time, your body would begin to look rather lopsided and strange. Together we are to give ourselves to loving God and loving each other. As a unified body, with Christ as the Head, we are to love others outside this community of faith in the hope that they will experience the love of Christ through us and even join us—because Christ's offer is for everyone (Ephesians 4:14–16). The Protestantism that drives American Christianity has a streak of "protesting" things like community. Our attitude is often one that promotes rugged individualism over community. When we open the New Testament, we often read it in light of our individualism, reading a "me theology" into what is written. We would do well to look at the perspective of our Catholic brothers and sisters who have historically read the Bible from a community perspective often called a "we theology." We are, after all, *created with a connection requirement.*

Evidence of the Connection Requirement

If it is true that God designed us with a connection requirement, then it would stand to reason that if someone were isolated from connection, it would have serious negative effects on his or her life. The American Institute of Stress has conducted extensive research on the role of social support in health. The findings are conclusive, incessant, and staggering. Directly off the pages of their research reports are these words: "The wisdom of the ages, anecdotal observations, careful clinical case studies and trials, epidemiological data on marriage, divorce and death, as well as sophisticated psychophysiological and laboratory testing—all confirm that strong social support is a powerful stress buster."[10] This summary statement basically says that it doesn't take a medical doctor to conclude that community is essential to life, but if you need this kind of evidence, they'll provide it in spades.

For example, careful research was conducted on 232 patients who had undergone cardiac surgery. Of these patients, twenty-one died within six months. Two statistically significant mortality predictors that emerged from these twenty-one cases were a "lack of participation in social or community groups, and the absence of strength and comfort from religion."[11] The medical community has pondered the strong connection between community and cardiovascular disease and concluded that wholesome community reduces hyperactive cardiovascular reactivity to stress.[12] When that community is spiritually based, health rises even further. Here is a scientific verification that God created us with a connection requirement.

Another example comes from a recent Swedish report that demonstrates that middle-aged men who had recently endured high levels of emotional stress but had little emotional support were three times as likely to die over the next seven years as those with close personal ties.[13] A California study involving seven thousand men and women found that after nine years those with the fewest social ties were twice as likely to die as those with the strongest ones.[14] The American Institute of Stress also cites a report indicating that social activity can predict cardiac mortality as strongly as elevated cholesterol and serum lipid patterns.[15] Research shows that "social support is linked with higher mortality rates for heart attacks, diabetes, rheumatoid arthritis and other autoimmune disorders."[16] Finally, another well-documented study shows that "social isolation contributes to illness and death as much as smoking."[17] So if you feel you must smoke, for goodness' sake, *don't do it alone!*

In this chapter we've learned that we are created with a connection requirement. After reading these first two chapters, many people will nod their heads in agreement, concluding that they possess the social support necessary to satisfy the divine requirement. Most people, as a matter of fact, might even conclude that companionship isn't their particular problem. We have people all around us.

In reality, though, it's possible to be in the company of others and still feel isolated. Community specialists call this brand of isolation experienced by the majority of Americans as "crowded loneliness." It is the most dangerous loneliness of all because it emits a false air of community that prevents us from diagnosing our dilemma correctly. We have exposure to people but not a deep connection to people. The truth is that there is a huge gap between God's original design for connection and the way most of us live our lives. Over the last fifty to seventy-five years, Americans and people from other advanced industrialized places either have never understood this design requirement or have downgraded it to an optional amenity. We must dissolve that gap and close it, or we will continue to struggle, suffer, and—I would even dare to suggest—die before our time.

My Thoughts on This Chapter

Small Group Discussion

❏ Using Genesis 2 as evidence, this chapter suggests that community is as important as air for human survival. Do you agree or disagree? Explain your answer.

❏ This chapter suggests that we need to make a shift from a lifestyle of accumulation to a lifestyle of conversation. Describe and discuss these two lifestyles.

❏ What makes a lifestyle of accumulation so attractive that we continue to pursue it beyond our means and beyond common sense?

❏ Do people really long for community and conversation? Do we not have it because we don't want it or because we don't know how to develop it? Discuss your answers.

❏ How do you feel about the evidence that the condition of a person's physical health is connected to their level of relational connectivity? Do you believe you or those in your network of relationships have physical problems because of a lack of significant community?

❏ Share your number one discovery from this chapter.

❏ Identify and share one personal action step you will take in making more room for life.

❏ Community-Building Exercise: Read the letter to the Ephesians together from a "we" perspective instead of a "me" perspective. Discuss your observations about the difference.

Personal Action Steps

THE SOLUTION:
Restructuring
Our Relationships
and Time

The solution to our problem of crowded loneliness involves a restructuring of our relationships and our time. Most of us know that something must be done, but we're at a loss as to what to do. In the following chapters you'll be introduced to ancient principles that work. Read on, O weary one. Help is on the way.

CHAPTER 3

The Secret of the Bedouin Shepherd

The Solution Is Not More of the Same

Several years ago I took my first trip to Israel. Our group traveled on a luxurious tour bus from one ancient city to the next, taking in the wonderful religious and spiritual sites of the Holy Land. In between the cities we would pass by hot, dry desert hills on the left and right. It appears to be the part of the Holy Land that the milk and honey never reached. Even though I was encased in an air-conditioned vehicle, my impulse was to reach for my bottled water and my fifty-block sunscreen.

Intermittently on these various hillsides were the shabby box tents of the Bedouin shepherds. I remember shaking my head and pondering how difficult life must be for them. Each of my four children has their own room equipped with gadgets too embarrassing to speak of here. As I gazed at the tents, they did not appear to have a 4/3/3 configuration (four bedrooms, three baths,

three-car garage). I remember studying about the Bedouin in seminary in connection with the little shepherd boy who found some of
the Dead Sea Scrolls in a cave in the ancient Qumran community
in 1947. The photographed faces of the men and women in the texts
I studied contained deep wrinkles parched by excessive exposure to
the sun. The gap in the way of life between those of us on the tour
bus and the Bedouin shepherds was enormous. I definitely felt I
was the privileged one.

Then our Arab-Christian tour guide grabbed the microphone
at the front of the bus and turned my world upside down. He said,
"Off to your right you will see the mobile residence of the Bedouin
shepherd and his family. Once their livestock has grazed the available vegetation, the family will pick up their humble homes and
move to a new place to repeat the cycle." He went on to say that *the
average Bedouin lives to be over one hundred years old!* Without
even meaning to, I blurted out, "How can this be?" Abed, the guide,
informed us of a study recently completed by the government of
Israel. They were just as curious about the Bedouin's longevity as I
was and wanted to get to the bottom of their secret, bottle it, and sell
it alongside the mineral-rich mud of the Dead Sea that promises to
create youthful skin. It was obvious by looking at them that the
Bedouin did not apply the mudpacks to their faces, but they did
something far better.

The first hunch was to study the diet of the Bedouin. While it
is true that their meals include whole foods, no preservatives, no
candy, and a moderate intake of meat, this was not the number one
cause of the Bedouin's longevity. Abed revealed the secret: *no stress.*

This makes complete sense! Stress makes us sick, drives us
crazy, and can kill us some thirty years before a poor shepherd dies
at the age of a hundred. Most Bedouin would not change places
with us, even if given the opportunity. And why would they? So they
can be stressed-out as they run hard to nowhere?

What does the average day in the life of the Bedouin family look
like? The family rises from their tents slightly before sunrise so they

are ready to capture the precious hours of sunlight. There is just enough sun peering over the horizon to see the objects in front of them. As the sun comes up, each member of the family has a job to do. Some tend the sheep—the core business of the Bedouin. Some make clothes or prepare for the upcoming meals. Some will mend with needle and thread the tears in the tents. At various intervals, the Bedouin make their way to town to barter the wool of their sheep for other staple items such as food and materials.

Whatever work to be accomplished is done during the day before the sun sets. There is no artificial light to expand the workday. Everyone gathers back to the cluster of tents—mother, father, children, grandparents, aunts, uncles. There are no television sets, no phone calls, no e-mails. Each night the family gathers for dinner. They are in no particular hurry. Often a fire is built and the Bedouin, young and old, gather around it. There may be music and singing, and stories from the past as well as stories of the day are told. Each evening can involve three to four hours of simply being together.

Because so much of the work of the Bedouin is physical, there is no need to squeeze in a trip to the gym across town or an appointment with a personal trainer. They are tired at the end of the day and routinely go to bed at the same time each night. As the young Bedouin shepherd boy lies down, all is quiet and peaceful; there is no incessant noise of city life to contend with. He peers up into the sky filled with constellations. Thoughts of a mighty God swim in his head. These will be his last thoughts as he falls asleep. Some say the slumber of the Bedouin is a deep replenishing sleep that eludes most "privileged" suburbanites.

Even now as I write this chapter it is Christmas Day, and I'm stuck in an airport in Charlotte, North Carolina, trying to get my family across the country from Texas to Ohio to be with our extended families for the holidays. We just received news that our flight has been cancelled. This is the second flight cancelled for us today. It's highly probable we'll spend the remainder of this special day right here in the airport.

I walked into a little bar and grill in the airport called "Cheers." Everything looks like it came right out of the set of the famous Boston sitcom. Only one problem: *nobody knew my name.* We were in a strange place, we had a fast-food dinner, and we didn't have a single family member in the entire state of North Carolina with whom to share Christmas. All this for a mere $1,800 in airfares. You really have to have a little discretionary money or air miles to ruin a great holiday. For some reason, I think the Bedouin shepherd would get a bigger laugh about my Christmas experience than anything Shelly Long ever said to Ted Danson!

The Bedouin do not live the hectic life of managing disconnected worlds of shallow linear relationships. There is a beautiful simplicity and a unity and rhythm with creation that extends their lives some thirty years beyond ours. They do not have access to our money or our medications. They have no need for them. The Bedouin are not the only people group that has discovered this kind of life—but it is a life that eludes the American suburbanite, almost as though we weren't invited to the meeting or didn't get the memo. Or could it be that we ignored it?

What is the secret of the Bedouin? The Bedouin approach *relationships* and *time* in a manner completely different from the way we do. This is their secret. It is a way of life that dances with the rhythm of creation. It is a way of life that is filled with a certain brand of community. It is a way of life that is free from the kind of stress we inflict on our lives and that creates all kinds of emotional and physical health problems that can take us out earlier than the master plan demands.

The way of life I speak of is as old as life itself. It sits plainly on the pages of the first two chapters of the Holy Bible. It is reinforced throughout the remainder of the Scriptures. Very seldom is it overtly discussed because it was the way life was established. People were born into it and didn't know to call it to our attention. They didn't "know that they knew." We, on the other hand, have lived most of our lives "not knowing that we did not know."

My goal for us is twofold: to get us to "know that we do not know" and then to move us to the point that we "know that we know." It is probably too optimistic to think that our generation can ever get to the stage of the people of the Bible or the Bedouin shepherd, where we "don't know that we know." But this way of life can be realized by ourselves personally and by the people around us if we have the vision and the courage.

Make this note: *This lifestyle can't be bought with money.* As a matter of fact, the excessive money of many Americans may be the single greatest obstacle to attaining a stress-free lifestyle. We can have the money to purchase the nicest and most exotic hammock made, but it doesn't mean that we'll find much rest in it. Who knows, if we point the next generation to the right path and attempt to actually live in community and reject crowded loneliness, perhaps their children will be rightfully called "the New Bedouin!"

My Thoughts on This Chapter

Small Group Discussion

❏ If you were counseling a friend who was stressed-out, how would you use the story of the Bedouin shepherd to encourage and guide her?

❏ Stress makes us sick and can even threaten our very existence. Discuss the stress points in your life and schedule right now. Do you believe that, if you don't resolve these issues, they'll be detrimental to your health? What are some workable solutions you could glean from this chapter?

❏ What will it take for Americans and others in modern cities around the world to make a change? Is it likely this will happen in your lifetime? Will you make changes, even if the rest of the people around you don't? Discuss some practical steps you could take.

❏ Share your number one discovery from this chapter.

❏ Identify and share one personal action step you will take in making more room for life.

❏ Community-Building Exercise: Go on an overnight camp-out in a nearby park or simply camp out in your backyard. If the weather doesn't cooperate, set up the sleeping bags in the living room. If you have small children, let them dress up for bed as they imagine shepherd children might dress.

Personal Action Steps

CHAPTER 4

The Circle of Life
Restructuring Our Relationships

The theme song of Disney's popular animated movie and Broadway play *The Lion King* is "Circle of Life." This song accurately depicts a beautiful way of life for the animal kingdom and a call to live in rhythm with the circles of life. There is the cycle of life and death; there is the cycle of the sunrise and the sunset. But there is another very important circle of life that deals with relationships and community. It's an axiom most Americans living in urban and suburban areas are completely unaware of and are violating to their detriment physically, emotionally, spiritually, and relationally.

Let me explain. Go to chapter 1 and find the diagram of the different worlds you and your family manage (page 19). It's not uncommon for a family of five to have thirty-plus different relationship groups to sustain. It doesn't take Dr. Phil to conclude that this pattern of life creates stress and discontentment. Consider for a moment that your drawing represents the life of someone who comes to you for advice on how to improve his or her situation. What would be your counsel to them?

Most likely you would use action words like *prioritize, eliminate, simplify,* and *consolidate.* This simple advice would be right on track and rooted in wisdom. Social specialists use a different language to say the same thing. They tell us that we need to exchange a host of *linear contacts* for a *circle of community.* For example, The American Institute of Stress physicians and sociologists tell us that it is possible to be in the company of others and still feel isolated. Why? Because many people have a large group of "friends," but in reality most of them are mere acquaintances.[18]

The Linear Model

What is the difference between linear contacts and a circle of community? Diagram the linear relationship theory, and it would probably resemble the drawing of your world. There is a relationship of some sort between you and another person (a *line* drawn to them), but they typically would not share a relationship with the other people in the other worlds you manage (they are not in the same *circle*).

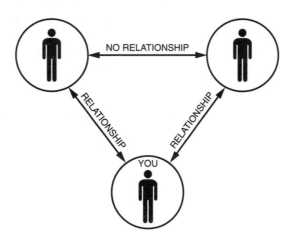

At first glance, this may not appear to be a serious problem. As a matter of fact, there may be some relationships you are obligated to maintain that you would rather not expose to your preferred relationships. While this separation may spare you some embarrassment and frustration, in the long run this may not be what's best for you.

In a linear relational model, you run from one relational unit to another. You go to work; you call your father or sibling on the cell phone; you golf on Saturday with a group of guys; you attend your son's soccer game; you meet with your financial adviser; you answer an e-mail from a former coworker; you go to church. As you exit one world and enter another, there may be some mention of the people you just left behind, but essentially they are not connected to the present world in any meaningful way.

To capture just how disconnected these worlds can be, imagine yourself inviting just one person from each world you manage to your next birthday party. You will go to bed that night utterly exhausted. Why? Because the only thing these people have in common is you. One lady recently did this and confessed to me that it was like keeping twenty separate plates spinning as she moved from room to room and person to person, trying to keep everyone happy.

The most damaging aspect of linear friendships is that no one really knows the real you. This can even include your mate, as he or she is often completely out of the loop on significant relationships you manage. I'd like to offer this thought: *a person doesn't really know you unless they know most of the people in your other circles.* Why? Because the most important thing about you is the relationships you have—your relationship with God and your relationship with others. For community to be authentic and strong, people have to share in those relationships with you.

In linear worlds your mate may not know much about the people you work with day in and day out. The women in your Bible study group may never see you relating to your children. In linear friendships you lack a group of people who know the *whole you* (your dreams, fears, hopes, quirks, and history—your unfolding story). Each world knows bits and pieces but doesn't share the big picture. And it really isn't feasible that they can. Linear friendships have some merit, such as a greater degree of privacy, an ability to exit one relationship without seriously affecting the others, and less accountability. But the downside far outweighs the few temporary temptations and benefits. Two-thirds of all people who struggle with stress cite loneliness as their major problem, even though hundreds of people surround them each day.[19] As mentioned in chapter 1, this is called *crowded loneliness*. In the end, the linear world leaves us isolated, misunderstood, exhausted, anxious, and shallow.

The Circle of Relationships

What the busy modern-day person needs in order to bring a deep sense of belonging to his or her life is a *circle of relationships*—a collection of people of all ages and stages who daily flow in and out of each other's lives. One of the secrets behind the success of this model of community is that the people not only know you but each other as well. It is an extended family of spiritual aunts, uncles, grandparents, nieces, and nephews who are committed to living out their faith in a simple, radical, and intentional way. This circle of friendships can also include those who don't live by faith in God but still share in the daily life experiences of a person. Together they share in the mundane exchanges of life: taking out the trash, checking each other's mail when the other is out of town, sharing the rental fee on a rototiller, playing a game of kickball in the street, watching a classic movie together—the list goes on.

At the top of the next page is a simple illustration of a circle of friends. Instead of the complex milieu of isolated relationships, which promotes crowded loneliness, we have a simple circle of relationships where people interact not only with you but also with each other. It is this approach to relationships that gives us the greatest chance of meeting the connection requirement discussed in chapter 2.

So much of the richness of life comes in the journey to the event, not in the event itself. Many of the experiences that make life sweet are the little nuggets and truffles that come our way when we least expect them. Read the gospels and you'll discover that many of Jesus' meaningful conversations with the disciples took place between events. In Old Testament times Moses instructed the Israelites that the most important lessons in life are best "caught" in the everyday movements of life rather than "taught" in formal events and classrooms.

> Hear, O Israel: The LORD our God, the LORD is one. Love the LORD your God with all your heart and with all your soul and with all your strength. These commandments that I give you today are to be upon your hearts. Impress them on your children. Talk about them when you sit at home and when you walk along the road, when you lie down and when you get up. Tie them as symbols on your hands and bind them on your foreheads. Write them on the doorframes of your houses and on your gates.
>
> Deuteronomy 6:4–9

One of the major problems with linear friendships in suburban America is that the relational opportunities in the journey to another place are eliminated. Each individual, isolated in an automobile, makes his or her way to the event, and thus so much is lost. The sayings of Solomon offer us this wise counsel: "Do not go to your brother's house when disaster strikes you—better a neighbor nearby than a brother far away" (Proverbs 27:10). In today's vernacular, Solomon is saying, "If you're having trouble and you have to get in a car to find help, you're in more trouble than you know."

This is the vision presented in *The Connecting Church*,[20] which recommends that we move beyond commuting to small group events in search of "contrived community" to living in a circle of relationships with the people nearby—the place where community can truly happen. How is this possible given the hectic lives we now live? The counsel presented at the beginning of the chapter is here applied. We prioritize, consolidate, eliminate, and simplify the linear worlds we have to the best of our ability, to the measure of our faith, and to the quota of our courage in order to create a circle of life. Dr. Paul Rosch of The American Institute of Stress drives home the importance of this concept by posing the question, "How many friends do you have?" Here are his thoughts:

> Before the agricultural revolution, isolated settlements probably consisted of about 100 people. Since these individuals probably had fairly close daily interactions, varying degrees of friendship probably developed among almost all of them. Interestingly, some authorities feel that 100 people is close to the maximum number of true friendships one can ever expect to develop in a lifetime. Today, some city dwellers may come into contact with up to 1,000 people in just one day. Many high schools in large cities have 5,000 students, or 50 times more people than our ancestors would have ever encountered in a lifetime! Sadly, although there are many more opportunities for establishing friendships today, it is equally apparent that less time is available to nurture them.[21]

Today we are overstimulated with people exposure, which affords us surface contact at best. This has many negative effects on our lives, including some of today's modern disorders and phobias.

Because we are inundated with the sight of people and "sound bite" contacts, we often don't see clearly that we need deep encounters with only a hundred people or less. Consider the average stop to get a tank filled with gas. You may see upwards to ten people and have zero contact with any of them as you dip your credit card into the machine and get on with your business.

Therapist Will Miller, author of *Refrigerator Rights*,[22] observes, "If you talk to any therapist today, the problems we see mostly are mood disorders: depression, anxiety, loneliness, and social detachment. As blessed as we are as Americans, as prosperous as we are, there's all this depression. So where is it coming from? I'm convinced it's rooted in the loss of 'refrigerator rights' relationships."[23] This is a delightfully clever way of describing a different kind of relationship. A person with refrigerator rights is someone who can come into our home and feel comfortable going to our refrigerator to make a sandwich without our permission. Miller argues that too many Americans suffer mentally and emotionally because they have too few of these kinds of relationships.

One of the major causes of a milieu of surface relationships and absence of deep relationships is mobility. Every year approximately 17 percent of the entire American population moves away from the people they know or are beginning to get to know—and it's been going on at this rate for at least the last ten to twelve years.[24] The mobility is often driven by the prospect of a more promising career or the desire for higher wages. Most people give little thought to the overall effect of these moves on their family's physical, emotional, and spiritual health. This game of musical careers is a key reason for the dominance of the linear relational model that is so debilitating.

The challenge is to find the center place that allows you to integrate as many relationships and activities as possible into a circle. Is there a way to bring the world of work, school, family, recreation, and church into one circle? For the Christian, is there a place where you can bring into one circle your relationships with believers in Christ and your relationships with those who don't believe?

While adopting this model of relationships may seem impossible or even a little "Mayberryish,"[25] it is the pressing issue to address. We cannot continue to deny that we were created for community and that the present-day linear structure is not meeting the requirements. It is pseudo-community, not real community. We must connect the dots between our lack of community and our declining health. Harvard Medical School professor Jacqueline Olds makes this pertinent observation:

> America is in the midst of a loneliness epidemic—and the isolation is undermining our health. . . . Our seeming obsession with the most intimate details of strangers' lives—as evidenced by the rise of "tell-all" television talk shows—is another manifestation of our isolation. When you lack a circle of people you know well, gossiping about strangers is a way to fill the gap. But it isn't very interesting.[26]

After years of searching full-time for the holy grail of community, I have found nothing as compelling as the neighborhood. Neighborhood or place-based community allows us to draw the greatest number of people into a circle—our spouse, children, other Christians, those who don't believe in or follow Jesus, older people, younger people, recreational or affinity friendships (golfing, vacation interests, hunting, reading groups, dog show enthusiasts, for example), and school friends. With a little intentionality it can also contain most of the activities we currently commute to—small groups, recreation, car pools, compassion projects to help the needy, and so on. Most important, neighborhood community enables us to park our cars and to see people between events, as we engage in our everyday activities. It is in these frequent and spontaneous encounters that so much of the richness of life is experienced. Apart from the neighborhood, these kinds of experiences are simply not available to us today without planning ahead.

The power of place-based community is that it creates the most tangible circle of relationships—the place where everyone of various ages and backgrounds knows you and can also know each other. While the neighborhood structures in suburbia are a far cry from those functioning for centuries in small villages around the world, which also included workplaces and marketplaces within that circle, it's still the best "center place" for facilitating community I know of.

When World War II ended, Massachusetts Institute of Technology converted former military barracks into tiny apartments for the ex-servicemen who attended the university. At the time researchers Leon Festinger, Stanley Schachter, and Kurt Back were studying attraction and liking, and they saw these apartments as a kind of laboratory in which to study friendship formation. After the students had been living in the apartments for a couple of months, the researchers asked them questions about how and with whom they had made friends, including certain things they might have in common, such as the branch of military they served in, their hobbies, their major in school, their hometown, and so on.

The researchers discovered that friendship wasn't based on any of these possible common attributes; rather, the biggest predictor was *proximity*—how close people lived to each other. Forty-one percent of the friends lived next door to each other, 22 percent lived two doors away, and only 10 percent of the friends lived on the opposite end of the floor. They called this finding "the proximity effect."[27]

This is not a new idea but one that has stood the test of time over the centuries. Those of us who live in the suburbs have lost our way through all the fascinating gadgets our minds and money have been able to create—things that have pulled us to and fro and isolated us from each other (suburban houses, select sports, the backyard oasis, automobiles, satellite television, air conditioning, and on and on it goes). But there are signs that this is changing. According to the Trends Research Institute in Rochester, New York, Americans are starting to "de-cocoon"—to come out of the self-sufficient homes they built in the suburbs and return to a connected life.[28]

Let's make an initial attempt to see if this could work for you. Take a sheet of paper and draw a single circle. Ideally, this circle would portray about a one-mile radius from your home. Now go back to your drawing in chapter 1, and see how many relationships and functions you can consolidate into this circle. At first it may seem impossible because you may not know anyone in your neighborhood or apartment complex. But what if you did? What if you made a commitment to park the car and hang out at home? What if you decided to participate in your hobby with others in your neighborhood who had a similar interest (golf, bowling, mechanics, cooking, dog shows, and so on)? What if your children concentrated on playing with kids in the neighborhood; after all, they probably already go to the same school? What if you worked it out to sign up for the same sports team? What if you carpooled to school and your kids' events? What if you invited empty nesters to your school's football game on an autumn Friday night? What if you had at least one meal a week with another family in the neighborhood?

How about a game night? What if you organized a simple night of pickup basketball every Thursday night in the neighborhood? What if you formed a small group with people in your neighborhood? What if your small group decided to reach out to the poor and needy around you—or visited the local nursing home once a month? What if you did a vacation or camping trip together? What if you planned a Fourth of July block party? What if you took walks through the neighborhood with those who were interested? What if you concentrated on sharing your faith with those neighbors you, your family, and other believers in your neighborhood were already connected to? What if you just enjoyed a simple conversation as you ran into each other taking out the trash or getting the mail? The possibilities are endless.

Here is some good news: This is a description of a *circle of relationships,* and it meets the connection requirement and eliminates crowded loneliness. But you may be thinking, *"I don't have time for this."* Don't be discouraged. The next chapter is going to lay out a new and simple vision for making time for relationships.

We must find our way back to the circle of relationships. Jesus said that you can't "pour new wine into old wineskins" (Matthew 9:17). But is it possible to pour old, vintage wine into new wineskins of the twenty-first century? I not only believe we can, but *we must!* So many highly successful people are like the Adam of old. They are sitting in beautiful surroundings with no care in the world when it comes to material things, but they're in deep trouble on the inside. They are suffering from isolation and loneliness. The superior design is to have a circle of friends in which people are not only connected to you but to each other as well. This garden of relationships provides a rich soil where roots can grow deep. If planted correctly, this principle of circular community can greatly simplify your life as well as add great meaning as each member takes in the communal oxygen God intended. The air of linear relationships is available— but toxic and harmful. It can give the sense that it is sustaining us relationally, but little by little we are being poisoned.

What are the practical steps to creating circles out of straight lines? I am excited about the words you're about to read in the following chapters. I offer you the hope of a "circle of life" to save you from crowded loneliness. In the words of a pig and a hyena from *The Lion King,* I wish for you *hakuna matata* ("no worries")—a reduction in stress and anxiety.

My Thoughts on This Chapter

Small Group Discussion

❏ Discuss the difference between linear contacts and a circle of community. Why is a circle of community recommended over linear contacts?

❏ Go around the room and count how many times each person has moved residences in the last ten years. How does the group compare against the national norm? Talk about the reasons for your moves and what you feel was gained and lost.

❏ What is the hardest thing you would face in consolidating your worlds? Brainstorm as a group possible solutions to these obstacles.

❏ To how many people with whom you have relationships have you granted "refrigerator rights"? Is this an invasion of privacy or an expression of intimacy?

❏ What do you think of the suggestion that the neighborhood is the best "center place" for community? What would change positively or negatively if all the members of your small group lived within walking distance of each other?

❏ Share your number one discovery from this chapter.

❏ Identify and share one personal action step you will take in making more room for life.

❏ Community-Building Exercise:

Idea 1: Recruit one volunteer from the group who would like to take a stab at consolidating his or her worlds into fewer circles. Work together on this assignment.

Idea 2: Ask each group member to consolidate one of his or her circles between now and the next small group gathering. At the next meeting discuss how it went.

Personal Action Steps

CHAPTER 5

The Hebrew Day Planner

Restructuring Our Time

The modern craze over the last twenty years or so is the day planner. With the rise of technology we now have the palm-sized personal digital assistant (PDA)—completely paperless, with access to the Internet. With these manual or electronic devices we can plan our lives away. We write down appointments and keep track of anniversaries and birthdays. With high-tech planning, you can put out many to-do lists, and whatever you don't get done will just scroll over to the next day and then the next until it is completed and marked off the list. The better, more intentional planning gurus even try to get you to schedule time and appointments in a way that achieves your personal goals. I think this is an improvement.

I like day planners and PDAs, even though I don't use one. I don't think they work, given the kind of lives we live. If the beginning of wisdom is to call something by its right name, then I don't think the best name is a day planner. We might call it a 24/7 planner. Or better yet, we might call it a "Chaos Manager." Connecting the popularity of the day planner with the discoveries we've made in the first four chapters, we might call the day planner an "Almanac for Managing Linear Worlds." The day planner is a tool to help us manage our exit from one world of people and projects into another world of people and projects within the same day. For the average American, this tool can help manage the entry into and exit out of five or six relational galaxies. If you are a mom or dad with active children, the day planner not only seeks to get the right child in the right place at the right time with the right chauffeur, but it also promises to keep you from leaving one stranded on an isolated relational island somewhere in town—how embarrassing would that be?

If you want to live a healthier, longer, and more meaningful life, a day planner is not your solution. Throughout history, people have seen no use for it. Certainly, the Bedouin shepherd's mom doesn't use a PDA. Can you imagine if she did?

"All right, family, as you go out into the fields to watch over the sheep, remember that I have dinner scheduled in my PDA for 6:00 P.M. sharp tonight."

The teenage shepherd boy and son would quip back, "Mom, why do you have to put that into that contraption? We have dinner every night at the same time. And we're always there, right on time!"

Today's mom scratches her head. This is certainly not the world in which she operates. She can't imagine her precious little shepherd boy not having slingshot practice after school or needing to be dropped off at and picked up from a birthday party for a shepherd friend three hills over.

While we may and can use a day planner to aid us in managing life, what we first need in advanced and more educated cultures is something more basic. Most people today have a daily and weekly pattern that is unbalanced and not sustainable over the long haul. I've suggested in previous chapters that if we continue to live this way, it will kill us. Not only are we not satisfying the connection requirement God created in us, but I'd also be so bold as to suggest that the way we plan our lives is the first obstacle to meeting this requirement.

I'd like to recommend to you an ancient concept that may be new to you. I'm calling it "the Hebrew Day Planner." This concept is rooted in the creation theology of Genesis 1 and 2. It goes back once again to our design as humans by our Creator—his specs on how we should function. In these two chapters of Scripture we are given the basic architecture for living a connected life. The Hebrew people were totally tuned in to these principles. It was the first story to be shared with their children around the fire at night.

The basic premise of the Hebrew Day Planner is that we were designed by God on the sixth day of creation to function in harmony and rhythm with what he created on the first five days. On the very first day God created light and darkness.

> And God said, "Let there be light," and there was light. God saw that the light was good, and he separated the light from the darkness. God called the light "day," and the darkness he called "night." And there was evening, and there was morning—the first day.
>
> Genesis 1:3–5

On the fourth day God filled the night and day with objects that governed the time of the day, the beginning and end of seasons, and the yearly calendar—in other words, a divine Rolex watch.

> And God said, "Let there be lights in the expanse of the sky to separate the day from the night, and let them serve as signs to mark seasons and days and years, and let them be lights in the expanse of the sky to give light on the earth." And it was so. God made two great lights—the greater light to govern the day and the lesser light to govern the night. He also made the stars. God set them in the expanse of the sky to give light on the earth, to govern

the day and the night, and to separate light from darkness. And God saw that it was good. And there was evening, and there was morning—the fourth day.

Genesis 1:14–19

On the sixth and final day of creation God made humans (Genesis 1:26–27). Now let's connect the dots. Do you think we were designed by God in any way to function in harmony with the creation? More specifically, do you think the *divine clock* of night and day has any bearing on our lives? I believe the answer is an unequivocal *yes.* I also believe the evidence reinforces this conclusion.

As we look at the pattern of the Hebrew day, we see that God's people have taken their cues from creation theology. Looking at the circle below we see that God has divided the twenty-four-hour day into two parts—night and day.

For the ancient Hebrew, there is a divine plumb line that governs the patterns of the day: 6:00 A.M. (dawn) and 6:00 P.M. (dusk). Oddly enough, the day begins for a Hebrew person the "day before," or at 6:00 P.M. This is consistent with the way God referred to each day in Genesis 1. After describing each day's creative work, the author of Genesis would conclude the section with these words, "And there was *evening,* and there was *morning*—the first [second, third, fourth, fifth, sixth] day" (Genesis 1:5, 8, 13, 19, 23, 31, emphasis added).

At first this may not seem like a big deal, but it says something about the priorities of God's chosen people, which we fail to understand today. We'll come back to this later. For now I suggest we focus on the principle that life for the Hebrew person transitioned on dawn and dusk.

There are essentially three major activities in each day that should be governed by night and day: *productivity, relationships,* and *sleep.* Because the work of the Hebrew was agrarian, productivity was accomplished during the hours of sunlight—6:00 A.M. to 6:00 P.M. At 6:00 P.M. the sun would set and darkness would begin to descend. From that point on, the time would be devoted to relationships—time with the family, extended family, and friends; sharing a meal; and a time of storytelling (no TV or Internet). This is where the Hebrew child would hear the creation story told over and over again. There would be no rush, because there was no place to go (no mobility). Between 9:00 P.M. and 10:00 P.M. everyone would settle down to get a good night's sleep. The basic structure of a normal day for the Hebrews went like this: twelve hours available for productivity and work (6:00 A.M.–6:00 P.M.); four hours available for relationships (6:00 P.M.–10:00 P.M.); and eight hours available for sleep (10:00 P.M.–6:00 A.M.). The illustration below describes this basic structure.

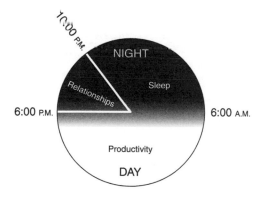

Each member of the Hebrew family would operate within these guidelines each day for six days (Sunday through Friday). On Friday at 6:00 P.M., the beginning of the seventh day, they would rest from their work (see Exodus 20:8–11, keeping the Sabbath day holy) in response to God's example.

> Thus the heavens and the earth were completed in all their vast array.
> By the seventh day God had finished the work he had been doing; *so on the seventh day he rested from all his work.* And God blessed the seventh day and made it holy, because on it he rested from all the work of creating that he had done.
>
> Genesis 2:1–3

God again reveals a key design requirement of the human model. We function at peak performance when we take one day a week to rest and replenish. If we violate this design, we are abusing our bodies and souls, and little by little we diminish our effectiveness. So important was this principle for living that God modeled it himself by taking the seventh day for rest. Did God do this because he was tired? Does divinity perspire? I don't think so. God did not come to nightfall on the sixth day and say, "Thank me it's Friday." God is reinforcing a pattern that is essential for healthy, productive living.

The central question is this: *Should we live by the same divine clock?* I think the answer is *yes!* We are humans born from the original design model of Adam. Archibald Hart uses the wonderful example of a machine. Most machines have a recommended "duty cycle" or recommended time they should be in service during the course of the day in order to run optimally. He poses this question: "What is the human body's duty cycle?" And then he goes on to make this observation:

> I am sure that people differ here, but in my opinion our duty cycle is 50 percent, like most machines. Why do I believe this? The

clues come from the natural cycle of day and night. We are supposed to work during the day and rest at night. What has messed up this cycle is the invention of the electric light bulb. Now our bodies no longer have a sense of daily rhythm—unless we give it to them.[29]

This is not a newfangled idea. It is rooted in the way life naturally functioned for thousands of years. In his latest writings on "The Next Society," Peter Drucker suggests that we're going to have to learn how to live in the places we've created for ourselves. He observes what we know all too well: "The twentieth century saw the rapid decline of the sector that has dominated society for ten thousand years: agriculture."[30]

We are living at the very beginning of a huge shift with regard to human existence, and it isn't all good. The agricultural lifestyle of the last ten thousand years naturally flowed, right in sync with the Hebrew Day Planner. The farmer would wake up in the morning in time to see the sunrise. He and his family would work during the precious hours of daylight. However, when the sun went down, the work in the field came to an end. With the animals comfortably stationed in their stalls or in the field, the farming family would enjoy an evening with a large, whole-food type of meal and good conversation, which is something people were much better at when television didn't exist. With the rise of radio they might enjoy an hour of storytelling or even a professional baseball game called over the airwaves. Everyone gathered in one room since the crazy idea of two or three living areas hadn't yet evolved. No one left the home in the evening to work out at the gym. During the daylight hours the farm provided all the aerobic exercise and muscle toning anyone could need. When it came time for bed, everyone slept well. It's the way life went for most people up until the twentieth century. Even in 1913 farm products accounted for 70 percent of world trade. Today it accounts for only 17 percent.[31] As Dorothy Gale once said in *The Wizard of Oz,* "Toto, I have a feeling we're not in Kansas anymore."

While there is nothing inherently or morally wrong with the shift from agriculture to industry to technology, there is something seriously at risk. In chapter 3 we discovered that poor Bedouin shepherds generally live thirty years longer than the average American. Their lives represent the simplest lifestyle of the agrarian society. This lifestyle flows most naturally with the creation theology of Genesis 1 or, as I'm calling it, the Hebrew Day Planner.

The life we've created for ourselves (or were involuntarily born into) does not naturally have these boundaries built into it. Because we are new at this frantic way of life—just the last hundred or so years—we don't have a good grasp on the overall impact it has on us as individuals. Significant results are now in, and there are, to be sure, many exciting aspects of living in a global society with unprecedented technological inventions. The rise of these inventions most brilliantly manifests the reality that we who are created in the image of God have an amazing ability to create. I am still utterly blown away when I talk to my father in Cleveland, Ohio, in real time, using a tiny little wireless contraption called a cell phone, while I am visiting someone in California. This is a beautiful thing—and is something to be celebrated.

However, we haven't been careful to monitor the effect these changes have on our need for community and balance. We live in a world that does not require boundaries. Night and day have been made nonissues in our 24/7 halogen bulb society. I can recall numerous occasions when I took my children to a professional baseball game during the last few hours of daylight. At about the seventh-inning stretch I looked up in the sky and realized that somewhere along the line it had become night, but I had missed it. With seamless precision the major-league-wattage lights came on and drowned out the darkness. As far as I was concerned, it was still daylight. While we can celebrate humanity's creative genius (still infinitely short of divine power, however), we must recognize that we've done all this with little regard for the connection requirement we discussed in chapter 2. This way of life may be wonderful in many ancillary ways, but it's killing us in the most basic of ways. We must wake up to this and make some serious adjustments.

I'm not suggesting that we all become farmers. Surely this wouldn't suit me well, given my childhood experience in industry-rich Cleveland, Ohio. I would be at a great disadvantage to provide for my family in a farmer's world, given my uncalloused hands and two theological degrees. I hardly know how to buy fruits and vegetables at the grocery store, let alone how to grow them from seeds. I know how to wring my hands in stress, but I don't have the stomach to wring the neck of a chicken in order to eat dinner tonight.

However, I am suggesting that we rediscover the beauty of the Hebrew Day Planner as a timeless principle for a healthy life and that we go on to engineer our lives in such a way that we readapt to its role in our lives. This is the divine plan established at creation to give us the room we need to live healthy, balanced lives. This, I think, is one of our most pressing issues. If we don't address it, we must not expect to ever truly live the life God intended us to experience.

Now take a deep breath and put the book down. Think about your life for a few moments. Think about how this divine plan might be achieved in your life. Then pick up the book again and read on, as I share my thoughts on how we can accomplish this in our lives today. If you don't have time right now, make sure you schedule some time in your day planner. This is too important to ignore!

|▌▌ My Thoughts on This Chapter ▌▌|

Small Group Discussion

❑ What method and products does each group member employ in order to manage his or her time, schedule, appointments, and to-do list? What works and what doesn't work?

❑ Do you believe we were created to conform to the divine clock of night and day? Why or why not?

❑ How does your current schedule compare with the Hebrew Day Planner?

❑ What changes or adjustments would you need to make in order to practice the Hebrew Day Planner?

❑ Share your number one discovery from this chapter.

❑ Identify and share one personal action step you will take in making more room for life.

❑ Community-Building Exercise: Invite each group member to try the Hebrew Day Planner format for one week and report back on how it went. (This works best if you keep a simple time log.)

Personal Action Steps

THE OBSTACLES:
Overcoming Bad Habits and Myths about Raising Children

There are at least two serious obstacles to overcome in our quest to make room for life. First, we must be fully aware of the *bad habits* we've developed that keep drawing us back into crisis mode and prevent us from enjoying the simple life of community. Second, we must address the *current myths* about how we're raising our children. Once we see the true impact our chaotic lifestyles are having on our children, we should be motivated to make the necessary changes.

CHAPTER 6

Getting Life Out of Balance

The Need for Boundaries

In the last few years I've taken up golf. I successfully avoided it for the first forty years of my life. My dad, an avid hunter and fisherman, always questioned the logic behind hitting a little ball and then chasing it, only to hit it and chase it again. He always said, "If you never hit it, you'd never have to chase it." But one day at a retreat I was compelled by my staff to get in a round of golf for the sake of team building. I didn't like the idea of playing a game I couldn't win, but I couldn't deny that team building was essential—so I went.

Things went pretty much like I thought they would—lousy! I even stopped keeping score. However, there was one swing of the club when everything came together for me (sadly, without my knowledge of what it was so I could reproduce it), and the ball just clipped off the club effortlessly and sailed high and long.

I've been hooked ever since. What I learned about that one successful swing, as I've tried over the last several years to make it more of a routine occurrence instead of a complete accident, is that golf requires two major things to come together simultaneously in order to hit the ball right: You must do the *right thing* at the *right time.* Golf not only requires perfect alignment, a proper grip, a good and proper takeaway and backswing, and a good forward motion and finish (the right thing), but it must all be done with a flawless tempo or rhythm (the right time). So it is with life. We must not only do the right thing, but we must learn to do it at the right time and with the right tempo—in rhythm with God's divine plan. Or to quote a wise simile from golf guru Bagger Vance (played by Will Smith in *The Legend of Bagger Vance*), "The rhythm of golf is like the rhythm of life."[32]

This sense of rhythm is not taught by many people. As we discovered in the last chapter, people for the last ten thousand years didn't think much about it. The life of the shepherd and farmer had built-in boundaries that kept activities and the lack of activity in proper tempo. So when the pattern of life changed during the industrial revolution and now the technological age, no one had a clue about how it would affect our tempo of life or our ability to do the right thing at the right time. Those who did have a hunch were ignored by the masses.

One of the most common mistakes in a golf swing is to bring the club down too fast. There is a false sense that the harder you swing the farther the ball will go. Nothing could be further from the truth. The downward swing of the club must be slow and in tempo with the rest of your body. When this happens, the ball goes effortlessly down the fairway. Archibald Hart makes this wise observation:

> Humans were designed for camel travel, but most people are now acting like supersonic jets. In a nutshell, most of us are living at too fast a pace. . . . The pace of modern life is stretching all of us

beyond our limits. And we are paying for this abuse in the hard
and painful currency of stress and anxiety—plain and simple.[33]

Most people believe that if we increase our speed, we will live happier and longer lives. This is simply not true. We must live our lives in tempo. This doesn't mean, however, that you'll get less done. Just as a rhythmic golf swing propels a golf ball, we can ultimately get further with a balanced life.

In the last chapter we discussed three major movements in the average person's day. There is *productivity*, or work; there is *relationship* time; and there is time for *sleep*. If we are going to make room for life, we must balance these three areas according to the tempo God created. However, most Americans live life out of balance in these three areas.

Work Imbalance

The Bible tells us that work is good and right. At creation, God gave men and women work to do with regard to managing his creation (Genesis 1:26). Solomon tells us that God gave us work to do and that we should enjoy it as a gift from God (Ecclesiastes 5:19). As a matter of fact, the Bible is pretty clear that the person who does not work should not eat (2 Thessalonians 3:10). The principles of the proverbs repeatedly proclaim to us that laziness is unacceptable and can only lead to poverty and impending doom (Proverbs 6:9–11; 19:15; 20:13).

However, God has set clear boundaries on our work. The Bible tells us (Genesis 2:2–3; Exodus 20:8–11; 23:12) that we should only work six straight days before we take a day for rest and replenishment. Jesus reminded us that we were not created for this principle, but that the principle was created for us (Mark 2:27). In other words, God created us with a duty cycle that requires us to be shut off one day a week. The Bible also tells us that too much work is not good. Solomon offers us these words of balance: "Better one handful with tranquillity than two handfuls with toil and chasing after the wind" (Ecclesiastes 4:6).

If work could be grabbed with our hands, we should seek to take only one fistful of work, and in the other we should grab a handful of tranquility. This is a fifty-fifty proposition. Fifty percent of our day should be given to work and production—this is good. Fifty percent of our day should be given to relationships and sleep—this is also good and necessary. It is a matter of balance.

You may be thinking, *"I get all the relational time I need at work."* This would seem to be a reasonable suggestion. Why can't we simply mix work with relationships and extend the time we work into the late hours of the night? For hard-driving individuals this appears to make sense. However, experts who study people who suffer from physical and emotional disorders suggest that the underlying source for their struggles is a lack of meaningful personal—as opposed to professional—relationships and support.[34]

Solomon tells the story of a wealthy man who is isolated and all alone. He has many possessions but can't seem to find peace with them. In a moment of dark despair the man cries out, "For whom am I toiling, . . . and why am I depriving myself of enjoyment?" Solomon concludes, "This too is meaningless—a miserable business!" (Ecclesiastes 4:8).

It is common in America for work not to be properly balanced. It's not that all people work hard or efficiently when they are on the job. Probably very few do. However, many people don't do their work within the boundaries God has provided. It seems that this principle is violated most flagrantly by the highly "successful," highly driven, type A personalities. This is the person many of us most want to become because he or she is the one who ends up with the most toys.

Accumulation is a full-fledged approach to life that is blindly addictive. Success is measured by how much you have accumulated compared to everyone else. It's how the game is played. Some call it "luxury fever." Solomon writes, "And I saw that all labor and all achievement spring from man's envy of his neighbor. This too is meaningless, a chasing after the wind" (Ecclesiastes 4:4). Yet not too many paragraphs later he writes, "I have seen another evil under the sun, and it weighs heavily on men: God gives a man wealth, possessions and honor, so that he lacks nothing his heart desires, but God does not enable him to enjoy them" (Ecclesiastes 6:1–2). Work is good—and even given to us as a gift from God—but when it is unbalanced with regard to the other necessities of life, something goes terribly wrong.

Work refers not merely to what we do at the office or factory. Work is activity and motion—yard work, exercise, children's sports, church meetings, and so on. In the previous chapter I suggested that we should work from sunrise to sunset—from 6:00 A.M. to 6:00 P.M. We should work our little hearts out during this season of the day. But when dusk hits, we need to be done with our work for the day.

When we work is one major issue, but *where* we work is another matter to be addressed. With the rise of the automobile and the superhighway system, Americans have the capability to live in a suburban area—where only houses, convenience stores, and restaurants exist—and get up each morning facing a thirty- to sixty-minute commute to work. In some places in the Northeast and on the west coast, the commutes can be up to ninety minutes each way. With the 8:30 A.M. to 6:00 P.M. workday as normative for most upwardly mobile people, one must leave the home at or before 7:00 A.M. and not get home until 7:00 or 7:30 each night. When we push the envelope beyond 6:00 P.M., our house can feel more like a hotel than a home. Hundreds of thousands of people each night find themselves in bumper-to-bumper traffic, thinking to themselves, *This is just the way the "good life" is.*

And this isn't the end of it. For the average family most evenings include running around town in the automobile for a variety of reasons—grocery shopping, church activities, children's sports practices or games, eating out, and so on. Not only has this running around seriously eaten into the family mealtime, but it has also extended our work and activity time beyond our duty cycle, thereby wearing on our physical, emotional, spiritual, and relational well-being. However, the negative effects are released only slowly, so that most people never really connect the dots between their work imbalance and their unhappiness and unhealthiness.

Relationship Imbalance

Not only is our work life unbalanced, but we also experience a serious imbalance in our relationship time. We simply don't get enough quality time with a close-knit group of people to meet the connection requirement. As we've seen, when the connection requirement isn't met over a period of time, things begin to unravel in all areas of our lives.

One of the reasons our relationship quota is not met is that our work responsibilities and our commute to and from work rob us of relational time. The best time slot during which to center in and focus on relationships is from 6:00 P.M. to 10:00 P.M. So important was this time for the Hebrew family of yesteryear that they started their day with the evening hours. The average American family simply isn't home in the evenings anymore. By the time we've finished working, driving back home, carting children back and forth to their late-afternoon and evening events, shopping, or working out, there's no time left for a full meal and meaningful conversation. No longer are mealtimes events but something we slip in between, or mostly during, activities. Because many in today's families are on such different schedules, everyone must learn to fend for himself or herself.

We haven't been taught the long-term value of sharing a meal and conversation at dusk; most people, therefore, believe that shoving a high-calorie, processed fast-food item down our throats while riding in a seven-passenger vehicle accomplishes the same end. It doesn't. We were born with the need to unpack our day within a circle of people who know us and deeply care about us. When we exchange this kind of simple existence for a motion-obsessed existence—which takes lots of discretionary money to pull off—new evils and new illnesses are birthed in our homes and in our bodies. Simply put, when our relationship time is unbalanced, life doesn't work.

Sleep Imbalance

Solomon tells us that "the sleep of a laborer is sweet" (Ecclesiastes 5:12). In other words, a good, hard, and honest day of work aids us in the sleep process. However, if this labor negates quality relationship time with a circle of family and friends, our sleep is drastically affected over time.

Sleep disorders have hit the American culture in epidemic proportions. Psychologist Archibald Hart drew this conclusion at the end of the twentieth century: "About half of all adult Americans cannot fall asleep at night. Forty-nine percent of American adults suffer some form of sleep-related problems such as insomnia. One in six American adults suffer from chronic insomnia."[35] This problem isn't solved by accumulation but by community. We can't solve the problem by purchasing the latest mattress used by NASA, goose-feathered pillows, silk sheets, down comforters, and mahogany poster beds. In the end the problem is the way we live our lives when we're awake.

Why is our sleep negatively affected when we miss the relational portion of our day? I come back to the divine clock that was set at creation. God has established our bodies in such a way that when the sun comes up, our bodies are stimulated to work. When the sun goes down, our bodies seek a transition out of the pressures of the day—pressures that are, in proper proportions, good and healthy—and into preparing for an evening of replenishing rest. How we use this time in between work and sleep is vitally important. If we press our bodies and minds to keep working, and if we keep making ourselves overstimulated and stressed-out—especially through driving around town to various events and activities, we will not be prepared for sleep.

Because I find the work of Archibald Hart so helpful, I'm going to summarize his thoughts from chapter 14 of *The Anxiety Cure*.[36] The center of our brain contains a "clock" called the *pineal gland* that accurately controls the rhythm of the brain. This brain clock is also the storehouse for serotonin. Serotonin is a God-given chemical that is released with precision and is responsible for ensuring that our body's physiology feels contentment and joy during the day hours. Not surprisingly, it works on the twenty-four-hour cycle of light and darkness. At a certain time each day the serotonin is converted to melatonin (now synthetically produced, interestingly enough, and sold as a sleep inducer), which sets us up for sleeping. At the onset of darkness—around 6:00 P.M.—the melatonin is released, setting us up for sleep. Melatonin is God's natural tranquilizer. At the onset of sunlight (6:00 A.M.), the melatonin is converted back to serotonin, preparing us for the day of work.

Whenever we artificially extend the daylight beyond God's creative design and bring the stress of labor or stimulated activity, which in turn releases the toxins of adrenaline, we neutralize the effects of the melatonin, thus creating a potential problem with regard to the quality of sleep. Hart writes, "High adrenaline, caused by overextension and stress, depletes the brain's natural tranquilizers and sets the stage for high anxiety." [37] If we continue to violate this brain clock cycle, it will cease to produce and release the required melatonin. We will then live in a constant state of inner stress and anxiety, which creates all sorts of problems and fears, including insomnia.

Many years ago Sir Francis Bacon made this insightful comment: "He that will not apply new remedies must expect new evils."[38] Americans cannot continue to live an unbalanced life, knowingly or unknowingly showing a disdain for God's design. We must make changes based on God's design, or we'll suffer the short-term and long-term consequences. We must make room for the life God intended us to live, not only because we desire it but also because it is essential for our continued existence.

Lack of sleep is not only the *effect* of living in stress but also (in some cases) the *cause* that throws other areas of our lives out of whack. Lack of sleep ultimately creates health problems that affect our productivity. We strive to extend the hours of daylight and starve ourselves of wonderful relationship time so we can get more done, but in the end it reduces our productivity. Also, lack of sleep can destroy relationships because it creates an internal imbalance that makes us unhappy, irritable people. Adding stress and irritability on top of our already depleted relationships makes even more elusive the chances of renewing them and getting them back on track.

All this may seem like theory—with too distant an application to interest the instant-gratification bent of the typical American— until you personally experience the crash. It happened to me several years ago and has stirred my passion for balance in my life.

There have been very few days that I've failed to thank God for leading me to become a pastor. There are so many aspects that totally fit who I am—writing, speaking, helping people develop spiritually, and being a part of building life-transforming biblical communities. In the not so distant past, I'd work all day, come home in the evening with a briefcase full of work, and retreat to a home office. I knew I needed—and wanted—to spend some time with my family, although I was at a loss as to what to do with them. Most nights at home together degenerated into watching television. Since each of us wanted to watch something different, three televisions often ran simultaneously. If at any time the family left to run an errand, I'd opt to stay home. As soon as they drove out of the driveway, I'd crack open the briefcase. I had already calculated what I was going to do. What's more, after all the family members went to bed and I had a brief conversation with my wife, I'd shake off the cobwebs and convince myself to go back to work. Many nights I'd stay up until 1:00 or 2:00 in the morning—a time I reserved for my creative thinking and writing projects. Being a minister can be very confusing because I could rationalize that I was doing my work for God and that this pleased him.

However, when you take a very strong passion for work and place no boundaries on it, something unexpected develops over time. I found myself unable to go to sleep. I'm not talking about going to sleep and then waking up and then going back to sleep again. I'm talking about never going to sleep. I had no answers as to why this was happening. I understood that people who were stressed-out and worried about their lives sometimes had trouble sleeping, but this wasn't the case for me. While my work has always been quite overwhelming—mostly because of my passion for excellence and my desire to bring things to completion—I hadn't been particularly worried or concerned.

It was then that I learned that a person can be stressed without being distressed. Stress, which depletes the natural brain tranquilizers, can be driven by an overextension of our passions and the things we love. I was available 24/7 to give myself to the things I was passionate about, and that became a problem. I don't think most of us truly know how much stress we continually live with, whether good stress or bad stress.

Each evening as bedtime approached, I would get nervous and begin to fret over the fact that I could not achieve the most basic activity in life—the nonactivity of sleep. I remember being wide-awake and strolling around in the house. *Surely I couldn't be the only one who was struggling in our family.* But I was. I would go by the bedside of my youngest son as he enjoyed a deep sleep, and I'd say to myself, *"How did he get better at this than me? When did I forget how to sleep?"* I felt so incompetent.

The pain didn't stop there. Not only did I experience a decrease in productivity and a sense of distance with regard to the affairs of my family and friends, but internal fears and anxieties started to emerge—and they had no content or logic to them. Without question, this was the most alarming season of my life. I thought I was losing my mind.

After a month or so of insomnia, I went to the doctor. (In my mind the fact that I put off going to the doctor sooner confirmed my manhood.) The doctor I was seeing at the time didn't know me—at least I didn't think he did. I was so embarrassed to tell a full-grown man that I couldn't sleep and was now scared to death. I certainly didn't want him to know that I was a pastor. I rehearsed my story a million times in my head. When the moment of confession came, I explained my situation and waited for the doctor to call in the men with the white jackets. He paused and then said, "When you add up the stress level that accompanies your job, caring for four kids, and your passion for excellence, it's not surprising this is happening to you."

"You know what I do?" I quipped back, hoping I had misheard him.

"You're the pastor of a large church in town. Most people know who you are." Oh, no, my cover was blown, but I did begin to feel that help might be on the way at last. My doctor told me that I was having sleep problems because of my lifestyle and that I needed to make changes. Jokingly, he said that if I moved to Borneo, I would sleep like a baby because the pace of life is so much slower there. I jotted down in my mental notepad a reminder to check on one-way airfares to Borneo. He prescribed a sleep medication for the next forty-five days while I would make life-changing adjustments.

This marked the beginning of the journey of installing the Hebrew Day Planner (see chapter 5) into my life. I traveled this road not from intrigue but from necessity. Because a low-stress lifestyle isn't taught in common places of learning or in the home, I had to go searching, and as I searched, some of the pieces started to come together. I entered into the phase of *knowing that I did not know how to live a balanced, connected life.* As I came to this point I experienced a rush of excitement and hope.

The process of installing the Hebrew Day Planner has been gradual but deliberate. One of the things I learned in my search is that Americans haven't been taught to live within any of the creation boundaries. I've also learned that Americans have carved a track of achievement and adrenaline highs that promotes this harmful pattern of life. Not every person in America suffers from what I'm writing about. Those who suffer the most seem to be those who drive hard to achieve a certain status in life and work. This conclusion, established by specialists, begins to explain why many of the illnesses and diseases caused by stress are unique to Americans.

While I want to achieve all that God wants me to achieve, and I surely do want my life to count, I've come to realize that God has established boundaries we must adhere to—a rhythm, if you would, that keeps us healthy, happy, and productive. When this rhythm is ignored, our relationships suffer. Based on the connection requirement, it is the most essential component of being human. When we starve ourselves of the "air of community," we begin to see new problems emerge: sleep disorders, anxiety disorders, irrational phobias, arrested productivity, and strained relationships.

Simply put, the American way of life is choking connectivity to others right out of our lives. If things stay as they are, the way we model for our children our approach to life will be to their demise. It is a way of life not taught with words in a classroom but caught as children live out a significant portion of their lives in the backseat of a van or SUV. In golf, the swing you take over and over again becomes a part of your muscle memory—your muscle performs the swing without conscious thought. By the way we live, we teach our children to establish either a bad swing or a good swing into their muscle-memory approach to life. (I'll deal with this in more detail in the next two chapters.) Once muscle memory is established, it takes a lot of work and concentration to change it. To remedy this social illness we'll need to look beyond the medications and monetary investments marketed to us everywhere.

As for me, I've never slept better, accomplished more, and enjoyed a more wonderful circle of relationships. While I have a ways to go, I strongly recommend that you install the Hebrew Day Planner into your life by virtue of the confidence I have in God's original design for us. You don't solve sleep problems by working on sleep but by balancing sleep time with work and relationships according to the brain clock given to us by God. I wish I could say the same thing about my golf game!

My Thoughts on This Chapter

Small Group Discussion

❏ Have each person rate himself or herself on how well he or she is doing at balancing work with other aspects of life. (Use a six-point scale: 1 = the most unbalanced, and 6 = the most balanced.) If you sense that your work is out of balance, is this an unusual season in your life, or is it quite common? Is this the way you think things will continue, or is there potential for change in the future?

❏ Have each person rate himself or herself on how well he or she is doing at balancing relationships with other aspects of life. (Use the same scale as above.) If you sense that your relationships are out of balance, is this an unusual season in your life, or is it quite common? Is this the way you think things will continue, or is there potential for change in the future?

❏ One-half of adult Americans struggle with sleep. Does anyone in your group struggle with sleep? To what do you attribute the lack of sleep? Could a possible cause be an imbalance of work with relationships or an imbalance of doing too much at night?

❏ The function of the pineal gland is a major argument in favor of the Hebrew Day Planner schedule (see chapter 5). Have a volunteer in the group explain how this gland works and its effect on us. What does each group member think about this?

❏ Share your number one discovery from this chapter.

❏ Identify and share one personal action step you will take in making more room for life.

❑ Community-Building Exercise: Pair up each group member. Have each pair share a prayer request with each other regarding their struggles with the above issues. Have each commit to pray for the other person once a day over the next week and to call each other at least once to see how things are going.

Personal Action Steps

CHAPTER 7

Childhood:
An Endangered
Species
How Our Lifestyles
Affect Our Children

Childhood is fast becoming an endangered species. Thankfully, some are beginning to recognize this and act before it's too late. *USA Today's* lead front-page story on March 26, 2002, was an article titled "Harried citizens take a night off":

> No homework, no practice, no clarinet lessons. No math league, no soccer, no SAT sessions. No swim meet, no Scout meet, no learning to sing. None of their usual sched uled things! Not tonight anyway, not in this town known for affluent, competitive, accomplished parents and children.
>
> It took a committee of eighteen people seven months and six meetings to plan it, but Ridgewood—where the calculus tutorial runs into the orthodontist appointment, followed immediately by the strength-training class—is finally taking what heretofore only a blizzard could impose: a night off.

The night had its genesis last year, when harried mother of three Marcia Marra realized how overscheduled her family was. She formed a committee to discuss the problem, and it talked about programs and discussion groups.

We said, "Wait, we're working against ourselves," says the Rev. Douglas Fromm. "Let's plan a night where nothing is planned."

The idea caught on, particularly after September 11, when the village of about 30,000 lost 12 residents. From a hill, you could see the World Trade Center fall. "People began to think about what is really important," Fromm says.

School officials promised a homework amnesty. Sports teams canceled games and practices. Churches called off evening classes.

Family Night's success will be measured only by each participant. Marra says, "We don't even want quality time; we just want more down time."

This being Ridgewood, someone asked for a list of suggested activities, but that was rejected as too well planned. And everyone laughed when someone else asked whether there'd be a prize for the family that had the best night off together.

"I hope they do it several times a year," says Noreen Romano, a psychologist with two teenagers. "Of course," she adds, "they'll have to schedule it into the calendar."[39]

This is a classic and common description of American life. The stronger the economic "advantage," as in Ridgewood, New Jersey, the more extreme the pace often is. As you read the testimony above, you see people running from one world of relationships and activities to another. Instead of centering down with a circle of family and neighbors during the relational season of the day, moms and dads are "dividing and conquering" in automobiles that cost more than the house my dad purchased in the 1970s. You will also note that, when the entire town decided to take a night off from all the activity, some didn't know what to do. While we can see that what we're doing is not healthy, we often continue doing it because it is what we know.

Humans are creatures of habit. When the Hebrews gained freedom from the hard life of slavery in Egypt and made their way to a new life of freedom, dignity, and blessing, they grumbled and wanted to go back to Egypt (Numbers 14:3–4). They knew how to do slavery—and they wanted to go back to familiar circumstances. They didn't know how to do freedom. I'm suggesting that we don't either. We are slaves to schedules, accumulation, and automobiles. A key observation is that this evening chaos is primarily driven by the children's activities. This is what I call "the juvenile suburban dance." Here's the primary question: *Is this what the children really want or need?*

I've been married to my high school sweetheart for over twenty years. We have four children whom we love deeply. When we began our family, as committed Christian parents we desired to go against the grain of "throwaway families" and "latchkey kids" and really invest in them. We wanted to be more involved than we perceived the previous generation to have been. How does one tangibly fulfill this mission? In suburbia the mission is to sign kids up for as many activities as possible so they'll be exposed to as many wonderful opportunities as possible in order to shape their self-esteem and future options. The theory preached to me by experienced parents of teenagers when my children were toddlers was to keep our children busy and off the streets. If you don't keep your children busy with activities that you control, they will certainly resort to drugs and gangs. We embraced this advice, and by the time our first child reached four years of age, we were running neck and neck with the best of the families in Ridgewood.

The different motivations swimming in our heads—and in the heads of other parents as we sat on benches at sporting events together—were driven with well-intentioned goals:

- *Children's activities are a way to teach your child socialization skills.* If children aren't involved in these activities, the argument goes, they will be outsiders socially, which will then get them connected to the wrong crowd and drastically lower their self-esteem—possibly the number one fear of parents today.

- *Organized activities develop our children in that particular area that will give them an edge later in life.* For example, you get your child started in soccer when she's four so that she can learn the skills needed to give her an edge in playing in high school. With suburban high schools now numbering in the thousands, only the very best get to play. Maybe, just maybe, she will shine and secure a soccer scholarship to a leading university. We want our children to do well. We also know that if they're going to sustain the lifestyle we've provided, they're going to have to be competitive and discover their unique approach to success.

- *Enrolling our children in various activities costs money and demonstrates that we're willing to invest our financial resources into our child's development.* Money flows toward priorities. When we sign up our children for these activities, we are communicating and confirming our priorities. For example, if you sign up your child for in-line hockey, you have league fees; the cost of in-line skates (which typically last for one season); the cost of pads, a helmet, and hockey sticks; the cost of trophies at season's end—no matter whether the kids won all of their games or none (in order to promote self-esteem apart from performance); and the cost of the coach's gift (not nearly enough to pay him back for managing the expectations of the parents involved). And don't forget another cost often overlooked when signing up your child for hockey: the cost of meals. Because sporting events invariably take place during the meal hour, you've got to factor in zipping through a fast-food drive-in window. By my conservative estimation and personal experience, it takes $350 per season per child to play in-line hockey. With the reality that most kids in suburbia are involved in three or four sports (most sports now have fall, spring, and summer leagues)—and usually some sort of nonsport activity (music lessons, cotillion, and so on)—it's not unrealistic for a family with four children to spend three thousand to ten thousand dollars a year in children's extracurricular activities alone—a figure not much lower than the annual salary level of those considered to be living in poverty in America. If you add select sports (a very expensive sports program that involves high commitment and travel), you'll pay somewhere between a thousand and three thousand dollars a year per child per sport. This kind of financial and time commitment allows us to believe we're serious about our children's well-being.

Here are two questions to ponder. First, *Are parents engaged in this excessive activity each evening because it's what they want to do?* While most of the parents I know would say they enjoy watching their children perform on the field, in their honest moments they'd confess that the excessiveness is really a sacrifice for the sake of their children's development. If you have a son who plays baseball, for example, it's likely they'll have three practices a week during the dinner hour and two games a week—five evenings each week for just one child participating in just one sport. The trouble with children's baseball games is that they take longer than most other sports. If your child plays the first game, you get to the field at 5:30 P.M. and are done at 7:45 and home at 8:30, as long as you don't stop for dinner. If your child plays the second game, beginning around 8:00 (on a school night), you get there at 7:30 and are done at 10:00 and home by 10:45. It's hard to believe that any parent really enjoys this way of life after spending a long day at the office or shop. However, because of the commitment we have to our children and because there's no other alternative to accomplish our goals, we allow it.

Here is the second question to ponder: *Is this really what the children want?* While children love to play and certainly enjoy some level of organized sports, I can't help but think that things have gotten out of hand. I believe that children prefer more hanging-out time, more unstructured time, more time with their parents at dinner versus having their parents sitting on bleachers at a ball field or in a gym. As I wrote this chapter, I watched my three boys play with three other boys (all different ages) out in the snow right in front of a friend's vacation home. Parents are not supervising or organizing the activity; the kids are making up the play as they go, according to ideas that occur to them. There has been a snowball fight and the building of a snowman and a snow fort. I just confirmed with my wife that they were outside for three hours. When I ask children, and even teens, their overwhelming vote is for open-ended, child-led, and unstructured time together.

The way that privileged suburban families are raising their children flows from a genuine love for their kids. Some of it may flow from the guilt of spending so many hours at work. Discretionary cash and two fully gassed vans or SUVs fund this strategy. While there are benefits derived and some memories gained, I would propose that this strategy takes away more from our children than it gives them. If we ever hope to truly make room for life, we need to rethink the way we're raising our children. If you believe this, won't you join me and the people of Ridgewood in making a change motivated by this same intense love for our kids?

My Thoughts on This Chapter

❏ What do you think about the residents of Ridgewood scheduling a night off? Can you envision this happening in your entire community? What would you do if everyone had the night off?

❏ Are the lifestyle and pace of the residents of Ridgewood similar to yours? Ask your group members who have children to share their daily and evening schedules.

❏ Three motivations are presented by the author for why we schedule so much activity for our children. Rank them in order of personally perceived importance. Explain your ranking.

❏ Children's lives today are overscheduled. Is this what the children really want? Explain your thoughts. Is this what the parents really want? Explain your thoughts.

❏ Share your number one discovery from this chapter.

❏ Identify and share one personal action step you will take in making more room for life.

❏ Community-Building Exercise: Pick an evening between now and the next meeting when everyone will take the night off, just like the people of Ridgewood did. Share your experiences at your next meeting.

Personal Action Steps

CHAPTER 8

The Lost Art of Play

Seven Ways Our Children Are Losing

I grew up on the east side of downtown Cleveland, Ohio. We were a lower middle-class family. We had one car, which my father took to work. Our activities as children involved playing in our neighborhood. No other options were available. One of our favorite activities was playing army. We didn't have plastic guns or helmets or even fatigues. Our guns were made of self-created carved branches. There were no pools in the backyard—and thus no fences or potential lawsuits. We would roam the neighborhood, hide in trees, and always argue that our imaginary bullet hit the enemy and that they should fall down and play dead.

Hours would fly by. The only thing that interrupted our play was dinner. When the sun began to settle we knew it was time to head home. All of our fathers were blue-collar union workers who worked up robust appetites during the day. Dinner was always served at the same time. Tardiness was unacceptable and was usually accompanied by a loving parental punishment.

Today's equivalent is quite impressive. When a child has a birthday, he invites all of his friends from all over the area to his party. The party is held in a child-designed entertainment center usually called something like "FunFest." Each invited child receives a token (at a cost of five dollars) to play a round of laser tag. Laser tag blows the doors off any neighborhood army. Each child enters into a dark room and is given a vest, which includes the target your opponent shoots at and a high-tech laser gun. Teams are divided into two— all assigned by adult employees. For fifteen or twenty minutes you run around in a dark room and shoot at each other and at other objects in order to collect points. There is no debate or conflict over who shot whom—the laser computer system referees that part of the game. At the end of the round each child receives an individualized computer printout that gives the team and individual scores. WOW! As a child, if I were given the choice of playing neighborhood army on Dover Avenue or playing laser tag at FunFest, I would have chosen laser tag at FunFest hands down! At least I would have the first dozen times. After that I think I might have opted for neighborhood army. I know my father would have.

Seven Deadly Sins

The way we are raising our children in stereotypical suburbia is taking its toll as we commit at least seven deadly sins against them. Dragging our children away from home in the late afternoon and evening hours to transport them to adult-driven, highly structured, age-graded activities has these negative effects.

Lost Creativity

Because adults organize most of these activities, children have lost the art of play or creativity in play. If a child has been raised with overextended and structured evening activities, they are ill equipped to know what to do if free time comes along. Because we buy houses today that store our stuff, and not homes nestled in a street-friendly neighborhood, many of our kids can't go outside and expect to play with kids in the neighborhood. In America it's likely that the majority of us don't know our neighbors well enough to feel comfortable with our kids playing with the neighbor kids. So our children are left to retreat to their rooms and watch television or play video games. Parents know this isn't a good thing, so they just keep doing what their discretionary money allows them to do. The result? Kids today are not as creative as kids in previous generations.

Lost Leadership Skills

Jill Steinberg, associate specialist in child development at the University of Wisconsin–Madison, writes the following:

> A lot of the activities that kids have access to are very highly struc-
> tured and not structured by kids themselves, but by adults, or the
> rules of the game. Normally, kids run games themselves if they
> are allowed to. But we've got them in structured day care and
> structured school settings. So they really have few opportunities
> to manage their activities on their own. But these are important
> experiences. By directing the activity, you learn how to negotiate
> rules. You learn to referee yourself. You learn how to take control
> and exercise leadership.[40]

The intent of today's style of suburban parental involvement is to show commitment, but we've forgotten to factor in the reality that our strategy would rob our children of leadership development.

Lost Mentoring

I grew up with a brother who is five years older than me. While there were a few times I threw things at him for picking on me, I looked up to him. When the kids in the neighborhood would organize a pickup baseball game in the parking lot of the farmers' market, my brother was usually a captain because he was older. As I remember, he always made sure I was picked for a team, even though I had little to offer. I watched him, mimicked him, and simply wanted to be like him. Because baseball requires a bunch of kids, our teams included kids of all ages. This kid-led, multigrade play created all kinds of opportunities for mentoring. While it's true that not everything we saw was the right or the best thing, for the most part the experience was very positive. (The same is true in the adult world of mentoring.) If something got out of hand, word quickly got back to the network of parents, and action was taken and the fear of God instilled—at least at my house.

One afternoon my friend and I (we were the same age) were hanging out in the farmers' market parking lot. An older kid approached us with a proposition. For every ball my friend or I hit over the fence he would give us a dollar. For every ball he hit over the fence we would give him fifty cents. This would have been a great deal if my friend or I was able to hit the ball over the fence, but neither of us could. Within fifteen or twenty minutes we were down fifteen dollars. It may not sound like a lot of money to the average kid today, but back in 1969 it was more than I had either on me or at home. I told this older and now scary creditor that I needed to go home and get the money—though I had no intent of coming back. I tucked myself into the innermost recesses of our duplex home and prayed. Within the hour I heard my dad call out my name from the front porch. As it is with neighborhoods where people actually spend most of their time at home, there is a network that makes it hard to hide. My dad paid the young man the portion ($7.50) I owed. As my brother watched, he shook his head and laughed, communicating to me with his eyes, *If I had been with you, this never would have happened.* Of course, it never happened again.

Today, most kids only play with children their own age under a concept that could be called "arranged friendships." You've heard of arranged marriages. Well, this is similar. For a seven-year-old girl to play with another seven-year-old girl in suburbia, "arrangements" have to be made by the adults. Telephone calls are made days in advance, drop-off and pick-up details are set. Because this "arrangement" often involves a commute across town, the subject of spending the night is often broached. This monogenerational play system involves a high commitment to scheduling and chauffeuring on the part of parents and wipes out the value that comes from intergenerational mentoring. Shame on us!

Because children today typically play with children their own age, they only know adults the approximate age of their own parents. This, too, is extremely unfortunate—as well as potentially harmful. Some of the most significant relationships and effective mentoring opportunities come with the "in-between ages." For example, my daughter has grown up interacting, hanging out, listening to music, going on vacations, sharing meals, and participating in activities with a neighborhood family group of adults and kids of all ages. She has developed significant relationships with other girls who are three to ten years younger than she is. It is a beautiful sight. It provides wonderful leadership mentoring opportunities for my daughter. This intergenerational community has enabled my daughter to grow up with spiritual grandparents, aunts, and uncles. In turn my wife and I have spiritual nieces and nephews of all ages.

I can usually spot a child who is fed an unbalanced diet of age and gender friendships. Their common traits are an intolerance for children of different ages and an inability to hold a conversation with adults—as well as a high level of discomfort in interactions with adults. They typically don't know how to share and can be downright rude. In my estimation, this is a direct outcome of an intentional parental strategy. The lifestyle many have selected for their children robs them of opportunities to experience and cultivate rich intergenerational mentoring relationships.

Lost Conflict Management Skills

In the same vein as a reduction in leadership skill development, activities driven, structured, and refereed by adults diminish opportunities for children to develop conflict management skills. If a conflict or tiff emerges on the playing field, the adults jump in quickly. Sometimes the adults handle it correctly; many times they handle it poorly, thus demonstrating that they haven't learned much about conflict management either. Many times I've seen screaming parents on the sidelines or in each other's faces at the soccer or baseball fields. There was even an episode of one dad killing another dad at their sons' hockey drills after the dads argued about rough play on the ice.[41] This kind of negative modeling imprints destructive mechanisms for conflict resolution on children's brains to their harm later in life.

In unstructured play, with adults nearby but not in charge, children are put in a position to resolve conflicts, at least with regard to the million minor skirmishes that emerge each day. If a child in a circle of friends continues to abuse the group and shows no sign of changing the behavior, he or she will eventually be shunned or not invited to the circle to play anymore. However, given a chance, children will learn how to resolve most conflicts in a sandbox, in the halls at school, or on the baseball field. This will serve them well later in life. Of course, Christian parental coaching and modeling are essential components of the equation. But this is not the same as directing and controlling the resolution of the conflict.

Lost Health

Medical doctor Paul Rosch writes, "Childhood, as we formerly recognized it, is rapidly becoming extinct. There is less and less free time for playing with others, and learning how to develop friendships and social skills."[42] I not only agree in principle, but I've also seen it with my own eyes. There is a certain sadness, and for some an almost zombielike state, in children today. The mystery and wonder of being a kid seem to be losing ground.

A whole new field of study has emerged and blossomed over the last ten years. The subject? Children and stress. An editor for *Healthy Kids* magazine writes, "Whether they're running off to child care, preschool, play dates, or after-school activities, many children today are overscheduled. While they undoubtedly benefit from a variety of activities, children can suffer from burnout and overcommitment and experience stress just like adults."[43]

The apostle Paul, author of thirteen New Testament books, writes these insightful and inspired words for modern-day parents: "'Everything is permissible for me'—but not everything is beneficial" (1 Corinthians 6:12). The variety of activities we arrange for our children is not immoral and is certainly permissible for the Christian parent. But not everything we involve our kids in is beneficial for them. As a matter of fact, if carried too far, which is the case with many children today, it can have long-term negative effects on their emotional and physical health.

Your four-year-old has preschool at 9:00 A.M., a play date at 1:00 P.M., an appointment with the dentist at 3:00 P.M., and karate lessons at 4:30 P.M. Child psychologist David Elkind offers this simple observation regarding this scenario: "Sometimes children's to-do lists seem as crammed as adults'." He goes on to offer this vital caution: "Overscheduling is a major cause of stress in kids. In the hustle and bustle, kids can miss out on two very important things—family time and solo playtime."[44]

Most parents I know—my wife and I included—have nothing but the best intentions with regard to their children, but they are unwittingly introducing their children to the same kind of stress they inflict on themselves. And, as we've seen in previous chapters, it has wreaked havoc on our lives physically and emotionally. Stress is now recognized as one of the key stimulators of cancer. This fact alone should cause us to stop and rethink the way we approach our children's schedule.

Because we are starting them earlier on this train wreck of stress, the results promise to be more devastating—a self-inflicted Armageddon if you would.

Lost Finances

I've already suggested that it takes a lot of cash to fund this paradigm of family life. The cost of purchasing and maintaining multiple family vehicles (including the gas to run them); the cost of the fees, supplies, and equipment to play sports; the cost of buying convenience dinners; and other miscellaneous costs all must be factored into the mix. But what does this have to do with the negative impact this lifestyle has on our children? Several things come to mind, but I'll focus on what I see as the main concern.

Funding all of the activities of the children can be stressful for parents to sustain. At Christmastime American parents often struggle to stay within a budget that matches their reasonably available income. Parents often struggle to restrain from excessive purchasing—they want their children to have a great Christmas. Stress becomes a reality when the December and January credit card bills arrive.

The same stress emerges out of a difficulty to say no to the myriad of activities we're invited to enroll our kids in. Once our children's world is framed in this method, it's difficult to exit, or "get out"—at least partly because there seems to be no other option. If we get out, and then find that we're not sufficiently convinced that the "road less traveled" is truly better, it may be hard to reenter the previous lifestyle once we stop. Our kid's spot on the team may be taken, or she may be significantly behind other children developmentally and thus find it more difficult to succeed or participate in the activity.

Most parents find it difficult to take this risk. So parents live with the stress of striving to finance the plan. Because this approach to budgeting isn't sustainable for the average single-income family, it often becomes a factor in a decision that both parents will work outside the home. When this happens, the parents often aren't available to be present at the activities—which almost guarantees the routine consumption of fast foods instead of wholesome meals that replenish the body. It also creates a chaos in scheduling, which raises the level of tension between Mom and Dad and the kids. The stress created by the financial burden is definitely felt by the children. Most of us know that minor discord between Mom and Dad is really a major stress creator for the children who observe the tension.

A simple game of organized baseball at 7:00 at night is hardly fair compensation for the number of impatient commands yelled at a child to get her to the event on time. I can't imagine it's much fun for the parents either. No, from experience I know it's not! And after saying all this, I have no idea how the single parent even begins to play this game—yet I am utterly amazed at how many do.

Jesus gives us this word of advice to consider: "Suppose one of you wants to build a tower. Will he not first sit down and estimate the cost to see if he has enough money to complete it?" (Luke 14:28). The real cost involves not only money but also time. Failure to adequately meet the cost, yet coupled with an unwillingness to get out, can send the cost soaring in the form of stress and chaos that rock our kids' worlds.

Lost Family Meals

Possibly the deadliest sin of all is not what overscheduling activities does to the child but what it keeps them from. In my decade-long study of human community, I've discovered that one of the very best things you can do for a child is to have consistent dinners as a family at dusk, with food that is balanced and whole and conversation that is free and slow. So convinced am I of this activity that I've devoted all of chapter 10 to it.

When I was a child, my mother always made dinner and had it on the table at the same time each day. I played summer baseball. I never remember our games or practices interfering with dinner. I don't remember a single time when my parents took us through a drive-up window for the sake of convenience. Today, children's activities have zero regard for family dinnertime.

Family dinner is not achieved simply by having food available for the family and then watching TV or departing to different rooms to eat. Nor does it just involve everybody sitting at a table together—although this is certainly a base requirement. Conducting family dinners is a lost art. It is the centerpiece of the day, the place where family and often friends sit down and talk, catch up on the day, and tell stories. The table is the heart of community. Yet most families struggle to have one dinner together a week, and when they do, they feel awkward, not sure what to do—and therefore they're not quick to repeat the experience.

In this chapter I've tried to demonstrate that the overcrowded schedule, which develops out of good intentions, is in the end very harmful to our children. It is not only stressful but robs them of the experience of the connection requirement discussed in chapter 2. If we genuinely love our children and want the best for them and believe that there's validity to what's been presented in this chapter, then we need to make a change.

I'm convinced that the Hebrew Day Planner model (presented in chapter 5) provides the outline for this change. Here's what it means in a nutshell: As a general rule, all children's activities take place Monday through Saturday from 6:00 A.M. to 6:00 P.M. After this time frame, work ceases, not only for the children but also for the parents. Each evening the family enjoys a dinner together, with guests invited from time to time. The cost of these meals comes from a small portion of the money saved from exiting all the previous activities. At dinner, the family and friends share the details of their day, laugh together, chew their food slowly, and tell stories. Everyone helps clean up the dinner dishes as an extension of the festival. After dinner, the conversation often continues. Some may go for a walk, a book may be read aloud or in private in the presence of others, a board game may be played, musical instruments may come out, and yes, some may watch TV for a little while. At around 10:00 P.M., the family, all accounted for, nestles under the covers for a peaceful night of sleep, excitedly anticipating the stories that will be told the next evening in the ongoing novel of family life.

My Thoughts on This Chapter

Small Group Discussion

❑ Discuss the ways children's activities and schedules have changed since you were a child. Do you think things are better, worse, or about the same? Explain.

❑ This chapter presents seven ways our children are losing valuable character-building experience today. Have each group member pick the one area that most connects with him or her and share a little about why or perhaps give an example of how it's affecting our children.

_____ Lost Creativity

_____ Lost Leadership Skills

_____ Lost Mentoring

_____ Lost Conflict Management Skills

_____ Lost Health

_____ Lost Finances

_____ Lost Family Meals

❑ Now go back through the seven ways our children are losing and turn them into positives—seven ways our children can win. Example: Change "Lost Creativity" to "Winning at Creativity." Identify at least one action step for each of the seven (for example, a pickup neighborhood basketball game can teach mentoring and leadership skills). Consider asking someone to write down and compile all the ideas on one page so you can share them with each other.

❑ Share your number one discovery from this chapter.

❑ Identify and share one personal action step you will take in making more room for life.

❑ Community-Building Exercise: Ask everyone to identify one of the ideas shared on how our children can win, and then ask them to practice it before you get together for your next meeting. Share your experience at the next meeting. (If you don't have children, consider doing this with grandchildren, nieces or nephews, or children in the neighborhood or at church.)

Personal Action Steps

THE HOW-TO'S:
Practical Steps to Making Room for Life

The "making room for life" vision holds the promise of a great life, but can it really happen, or is this just wishful thinking? The chapters you are about to read will give you practical ideas for making this a reality. Turn the page and get ready for action.

CHAPTER 9

Ten Principles of Productivity
Getting Work Done at Work

Night after night a man came home to his family with his briefcase full of work. One evening his little son turned to his mom as his dad once again walked in with an overstuffed briefcase in hand. "Why does Daddy always have work to do when he gets home?" he asked. His mom replied, "Because Daddy can't get it all done at the office." The boy innocently quipped back, "Why don't they put Daddy in the slower class?"

We've already established in chapter 5 that work is a very important part of our life. It is good, and it is from God. However, our work must be kept in balance with the time we take for relationships and for sleep in order for us to live healthy, happy lives. In James Patterson's best-selling novel *Suzanne's Diary for Nicholas*— the story of a busy mother and doctor named Suzanne, who is terminally ill because of a heart condition—we learn how Suzanne makes dramatic changes to structure her life in a way that balances work with relationships. As expected, she dies at a young age, and eventually her husband remarries. The stepmother finds a diary that Suzanne kept for her son, Nicholas. In the diary she finds these words of wisdom:

> Imagine life is a game in which you are juggling five balls. The balls are called work, family, health, friends, and integrity. And you're keeping all of them in the air. But one day you finally come to understand that work is a rubber ball. If you drop it, it will bounce back. The other four balls—family, health, friends, and integrity—are made of glass. If you drop one of these, it will be irrevocably scuffed, nicked, or perhaps even shattered. And once you truly understand the lesson of the five balls, you will have the beginnings of balance in your life.[45]

The Hebrew Day Planner suggests that we have twelve hours of work time available to us—beginning when you get out of bed and ending when you arrive home. This means that 50 percent of a twenty-four-hour day is available for work and productivity—which seems like a reasonable and generous chunk of time. However, work is one of the top predators of community (overscheduling our evening hours with children's activities is either number one or number two to work); it preys on those precious few hours in the evening when we can be with a circle of family and friends. I'm hopeful that by now you are utterly convinced that this brand of circular social interaction is critical to your life.

Is it really possible that we can learn how to get our work done in this time frame? I'd like to suggest some practical principles of productivity that may help this become a reality for you. Keep in mind that these are principles that must be learned and applied in order for them to have their full impact. Also, not every principle will be possible for everyone, given the jobs you currently have. Therefore, you may want to prioritize these in the order in which you wish to or are able to implement them, starting with the one that could have the greatest impact, given your situation.

The Principle of Goal Setting

Setting work and career goals is a double-edged sword. In the most obvious way it creates motivation for productivity and effectiveness. In a less obvious way, goal setting can provide boundaries and limits. When we go to work with well-defined goals, we have specific things to achieve. We are on a mission. When these things are being achieved in a reasonable time frame, we can pace ourselves in such a way so as to not burn the candle at both ends of the day—actually on either end of the day.

Effective goal setting doesn't end with establishing a goal but also includes the logical steps necessary to accomplish the goal. When we lay out more specific steps, we don't have to feel so overwhelmed with regard to the achievement of the goal.

Someone once wisely stated that "the journey of a million miles begins with but one step." I find that people who have hefty and lofty goals but who have failed to break them into bite-size daily steps often wander inefficiently through a day. This poor planning usually creates stress because work ends up having to be done in too short a time. Without question, well-defined goals can be used not only to get work accomplished but also to get you home on time.

If you work for someone, you should go over these goals ahead of time with him or her to make sure that both of you are on the same page in terms of production, quantity, and quality. Also, make sure you share your desire to be a serious contributor to the success of the company, but also be clear that you want to balance your work with your commitments to family and friends. Explain your desire to be home no later than 6:00 P.M. every night. Establishing well-defined goals and then measuring your accomplishment of these goals should help your supervisor work with you toward this worthy and balanced vision.

I work for a board of seven to nine individuals. Over the last several years we've moved to a system of accountability through goals rather than hours on the clock. At the beginning of the year I present a list of goals I will seek to accomplish. Once these are approved, I can go to work. I now have the freedom to manage my work in such a way that I provide excellent service as well as pace myself each day to ensure that there is room for a healthy dose of community and conversation. For example, we've established ahead of time that I will preach on thirty-five of the fifty-two Sundays in a calendar year. On each of these thirty-five weeks, preparing a quality sermon is a top priority.

The Principle of the To-Do List

Having well-defined goals that are approved by your supervisor, accompanied by the intent to achieve the goals with excellence and in a timely manner, opens the door to getting home at or before 6:00 P.M. However, we must go one step further. We must create a daily to-do list from these stated goals a day or even a week in advance.

One member of my congregation has lived the Hebrew Day Planner concept religiously for years. One of the things he's done masterfully is writing down the top three things he must get done the next day during the work hours of daylight. He doesn't use a PDA but rather a simple 3x5 card. When he's done with these three items, he's done working for the day. Because these things are carefully chosen the day before and because he is very disciplined, he seems to never struggle to be done by 6:00 P.M. As a matter of fact, he's usually done before noon. After knowing this man for twenty years, I believe he may be the most successful, de-stressed person I know.

Be careful not to dismiss this principle just because you don't feel you have this kind of freedom. We can all learn from this productivity principle, no matter what job we hold. I mentioned above that I have a shared goal with my church's elder council that I will speak a minimum of thirty-five Sunday mornings a year. Because this is my number one job responsibility, it is the first item on my to-do list for Monday morning. I stay home so that I'll avoid highly stimulating conversations with my staff members. Eight out of ten times, the sermon is done by the end of the working day on Monday (6:00 P.M.). On at least five of these occasions, the sermon is completed by 2:00 P.M. I spent the first eight years of pastoral ministry on a schedule that would get me home well after 6:00 P.M. and would leave me stressed-out at the end of the week—often, in fact, without a sermon! The irony was that on Sunday morning I was going to stand up and tell my congregation how to live the Christian life, and yet on Monday through Saturday night my attitude suggested I knew very little about the subject.

Writing out a to-do list is an age-old practice that most of my friends and acquaintances don't do very well. However, the goal in this book is not to become proficient at establishing a highly honed to-do list the day before so that you can get more work done in a given day. Rather, the goal is to be a responsible steward for God, your employer, and your family by being productive during the work hours so you can be faithful to enter into the relationship season (6:00 P.M.–10:00 P.M.) successfully without feeling guilty.

The Four-Hour Principle

Specialists tell us that the most gifted of us only get a total of four hours of effective work done in any given day. While we may spend eight, ten, or twelve hours at the office, when all the chaff is separated from the pure wheat, there are only four hours worth of highly productive labor on the table. (I personally think that four hours may be a bit too generous.)

How does this principle help us live out the Hebrew Day Planner more consistently? If embraced, it dispels the notion that spending more time in the office is the solution to our productivity problems. Many people believe they're showing that they take their work seriously if they stay longer at the workplace. This is simply not true. Rather, we should seek to consolidate our four hours of effective work within the tightest framework we can—six to eight hours certainly seems achievable.

The Principle of Giftedness

One of two principles seems to be at work: (1) Because there are areas of my job where I am not gifted, time flows toward my weaknesses and I seldom get to do what I am truly gifted at doing. (2) My time flows toward what I am gifted in and passionate about, but because my job includes more than this, I am constantly falling behind and getting stressed-out. Either one of these scenarios can leave a person feeling overworked and overwhelmed. In order to balance your work with your relationships and your sleep time, you must find some remedy.

The ideal solution is to define as much of your job as you can in your realm of giftedness. The thought is simple: You are the most valuable and productive when you work in your area of giftedness. The second justification is that you are the most fulfilled and efficient when you work within the scope of your giftedness.

Here's the challenge with this principle: How do you identify the center of your giftedness and find a job that needs what you do best and pays you a decent wage to do it? If you are able to put this principle into practice in your life, you should enter corporate worship each Sunday with a grateful heart, eager to express your worship and bring your financial gifts to God, because very few people are able to make this principle work.

However, you must be careful to place boundaries on the amount of work you do under this arrangement. The more passionate you are about your work and the more praise you receive from others, the greater the temptation to extend the time you spend doing it. Our human nature causes us to move toward that which we feel competent doing. If you currently feel awkward and unsuccessful around your family and friends, you may subconsciously avoid the extensive encounters recommended by the Hebrew Day Planner. This should not encourage us to move away from the principle of giftedness, but we should seek to use it wisely to encourage balance in our lives.

Applying the first four principles of productivity would read like this: (1) We should seek to work the greatest portion of our day within our area of giftedness; (2) we should mutually agree on our goals with our supervisor or board; (3) the day before we come to work, we should develop the top three or four things we need to do to achieve our goals; and (4) what we plan to accomplish should be reasonably achieved in four hours, leaving additional time if necessary for unavoidable distractions, breaks, and administrative requirements.

The Principle of Delegation and Teamwork

This principle of productivity, if effectively applied, can aid us in getting all of the necessary work done within a healthy allotment of time (6:00 A.M.–6:00 P.M.). If teamwork could be formed on the basis of a balance of gifts, and if everyone knew and respected each other's gifts and unique contribution, more work could be done in less time.

Three things need to happen in order for this principle to be activated. First, we must know our own gifts and competencies. Second, we must know the gifts and competencies of each member of our team. Third, we must organize and delegate the work to be done according to this giftedness and commitment to teamwork. It would be wise for every team to discover and apply these necessary steps. When applied, this plan yields intense productivity.

It has been my experience that every effective team needs three kinds of workers: influencers, contributors, and managers. Influencers create and cast vision. Contributors do the frontline work. Managers train, equip, and support the team of contributors to get the work done. When a team has people placed according to their design, productivity skyrockets. When people are placed out of whack with their giftedness, no number of hours invested will allow a team to experience long-term economic or missional viability.

The Principle of Positional Identity

The classic movie *Chariots of Fire* tells the story of two men who competed in the 1924 summer Olympics and won gold medals (Harold Abrahams in the 100-meter race and Eric Liddell in the 400-meter race). However, they ran for different reasons. Abrahams ran to prove to himself and to the world that he was someone who should be taken seriously. This is understandable, given the difficulty Jewish people had in being accepted in Christian cultures of the 1930s. But what a stressful way to live. Eric Liddell, on the other hand, ran to express who he was. He is quoted as saying, "When I run, I feel God's pleasure."

Liddell is expressing one of the most powerful benefits of the Christian life—the principle of positional identity. This axiom of faith is built on the foundation that, when a person believes in and receives Jesus Christ as Savior, he or she becomes a child of God (John 1:12). This new identity is not granted because of our performance but because of the perfect performance of Jesus on our behalf (John 3:16; Ephesians 2:8–9). If the Christian disciple comes to understand and embrace this principle as a way of life, it will dramatically affect his or her work life. Each morning as we wake up to face the day, the issue of *who we are* is not up for grabs. Our mission becomes to *express* who we are, not to *prove* to others who we are.

How does this principle work to make us more productive? When a person is secure in who he or she is and positively seeks to express it through work, there is a greater likelihood of avoiding addiction to work, praise, or competition, as well as the unhealthy climbing of the corporate ladder in an area outside of our gifted-ness. For those who look to their work for a sense of identity (instead of expressing their identity through their work), their lives can become as pitiful as that of dogs begging for table scraps. It is a shameless pursuit. Many people in this position—or lack of posi-tion—struggle to keep their work life in balance with cultivating relationships and getting the necessary sleep.

The Principle of Commute Reduction

The Hebrew Day Planner architecture calls for production to be done from 6:00 A.M. to 6:00 P.M. Included in this block of time is the commute to and from work. With many people experiencing one hour commutes each way, it makes it difficult to get to work, do the work expected of you, and return home—all by 6:00 P.M. I see five possible solutions:

Move Closer to Work

Over the last fourteen years my family has made a commitment to consider our places of work in our selection of a home. We've lived in two places in the same town during these years, and both of these places have been less than five miles from my office. This has not only reduced the stress of traffic jams and road rage but has also added to my available time for work one to three hours a day, or up to fifteen hours a week.

Go to and Leave Work When Traffic Is Light

In my town, if you want to head into Dallas from Arlington, you need to leave either before 6:30 A.M. or after 8:45 A.M. The same principle applies on the way home: leave either at or before 4:00 P.M. or wait until after 6:30 P.M. Of course, I'm in favor of leaving early and coming home early in order to meet the requirement of the Hebrew Day Planner. Talk to your supervisor and see if you can work out a suitable arrangement. Many companies already utilize flextime, which makes it easy for the employee to adjust to the Hebrew Day Planner.

Use Public Transportation

Many suburbs have a train, subway, or busing system that allows you to ride on a strict schedule and get work done while traveling both to and from your office. The key is to follow a schedule, reserving for the commute the kind of work you can do on a train.

Work at Home

This may not sound like an attractive option to many of you, but you may want to consider it as the lesser of two evils—scrambling like crazy to try to be home at 6:00 P.M. and avoiding stress-filled traffic jams, or finding a quiet and motivating spot to work at home. More and more companies are providing this option as a way to reduce the overhead cost of office space. Certain cities in California, such as in the Silicon Valley area, are offering tax incentives to companies who can keep their employees off the already supercongested roadway system. Look for planned communities in the near future that promote this feature of working at home or in an office complex within walking distance of many homes.

If you can't work at home every day, see if you can do it two or three days a week. Don't be surprised to discover the same thing homeschoolers have discovered: *It doesn't take all day to get your work done.* Many reasonably disciplined children who are home-schooled get their work done by noon or 1:00 P.M. each day. Studies show that a great number of them are outstripping their conventional schoolmates in academic achievements and are being admitted into North America's top colleges and universities.

Change Jobs

This may sound crazy—and it may not be possible—but don't dismiss it too quickly. If you embrace the need to shift from a lifestyle of accumulation to a lifestyle of conversation, and if you chose your job because of the compensation that would allow you to finance a chosen consumer lifestyle, then it makes sense that you would reconsider your decision if the premise changed. At the very least, if commuting long distances each day is an issue for you and you can't apply the first four ideas, this is something that deserves being put on the table and seriously considered. Insanity is doing the same thing over and over again, expecting all the while vastly different results. Do something different for a change.

The Principle of Results for Flexibility

This principle has already been expressed above in the example of seeking permission to reduce your commute time by changing the times you go to and leave the office in order to avoid traffic congestion. However, this principle is significant enough to deserve its own space.

My assistant works full-time. She is married and has a fifteen-year-old daughter. I want to see her live a balanced life, and therefore I'm open to this principle. She promises to deliver defined results while I offer her flexibility. We have worked out the following arrangement: She drops her daughter off at school at 7:30 A.M. and gets to the office at 7:45. On Tuesday, Wednesday, and Thursday her goal is to leave at 5:30 P.M. If she accomplishes what she needs to get done for that day, she sometimes leaves earlier, which I support. On Monday and Friday she leaves at 2:30 P.M. to pick up her daughter from school. If she still has a few things to get done, she'll plan her day so that it can be done at home. However, our goal is for her to be done for the day at 2:30. When you have a person with her outstanding work ethic and ability to manage priorities, a boss would be a fool to forbid this structure. At the end of the day she feels in charge of her life and refreshed, grateful to have the opportunity to enjoy the work God has given her to do while balancing work with relationships of family and friends and the need for sleep. Results-oriented people are the kind of people bosses should seek to hire; every employee should seek to be a results-oriented person.

The Principle of Outsourcing

I have a wife and four children. My wife and I began to notice that, as we looked at our schedule from week to week, there were two time-consuming things left on the agenda that we wanted to eliminate. Don't be shocked at its uniqueness: doing the yard work and cleaning the house. What if we could outsource these tasks? Impossible! After all, that's only available to the superrich. While this suggestion is out of the reach for some at certain seasons of life (like college students—who probably don't own houses with lawns—or possibly newlyweds), it deserves consideration if we want to make the shift from accumulation to conversation and still live in suburbia.

Here's what we came up with as a solution. The average monthly car payment in our area is around $400 a month. For a large family like ours, the cost of a seven- or eight-passenger vehicle can easily be $700 or $800 a month. What if we diligently saved enough money to pay cash for a reliable used car (reliable to us means that it can have high miles, as long as it's been well serviced and has records to prove it), and then used the freed-up cash to purchase time? While it may differ from community to community, we've been able to find excellent services to clean our house once a week and to care for our lawn once a week for around $400 a month. Because our commuting is drastically less than the average family, the used, paid-off cars we drive, if routinely serviced, do a fine job of getting us from point A to point B.

Why do outsourcing services such as housecleaning and yard work sound lavish and pretentious but owning a brand-new automobile that depreciates in value daily seem like an nonnegotiable purchase and the inalienable right of all Americans? I would like to suggest that the journey of making room for life—of moving from accumulation to conversation—sees things differently.

The Principle of Efficiency

This final principle, while self-evident, if practiced will do as much as any of the other principles to make us more productive in less time so that we can daily experience the kind of relational community we were designed to experience.

The principle of efficiency essentially seeks to perpetually answer this question about all we do at work: *How can this be done in less time?* This may not apply to the aging of wine, but it applies to most things I can think of that must be done in the workplace. Simply make a list of the things you do, and seek to find a more efficient way to do it. I recommend that you seek counsel from others.

I once heard the true story of a man who decided to go to his annual homeowners' association meeting. They were having problems with beavers eating the trees. A motion was made by the chairperson to replace the trees eaten by the beavers. How crazy! The only reason you'd want to do this is if you had a mission to feed the lifestyle of beavers. But if your desire is to efficiently solve this problem, the correct solution is to refrain from planting trees until you take care of the beavers.

My wife and I purchased our first washer and dryer in 1983 when we bought our first home. With routine maintenance these appliances were still running twenty years later. With a family of six, washing clothes is a major chore and a significant investment of time. My wife's biggest problem was that she was having to run the dryer for two or three complete cycles in order for the clothes to dry, which involved a lot of waiting and a lot of stress. Because we don't do work in our home after 6:00 P.M.—including washing clothes—we decided we needed to look for a solution to this problem.

We zeroed in on the pursuit of efficiency as a potential answer. We discovered that it was possible to buy a new washer and dryer for about the same price we paid for our current set. However, it would result in just a slight improvement. We then found a set that cost twice the money, but it claimed to use less water during the washing cycle so that the clothes weren't as wet when put into the new, more powerful, efficient dryers. The sales pitch was that the dryer would be done drying before the next load of clothes was done washing. That was just what we were looking for!

So in the course of considering the purchase, we checked with some people who owned this particular set to see if the salesperson was giving us the true story. To our amazement he was. I took a calculator and determined that our current set was costing us about $40 a year. Using the same formula we concluded that the new set would cost us $80 a year, or $1.54 cents a week. Here was the deciding question: *Would we be willing to spend $1.54 a week for my wife and the mother of four children to gain back twelve hours of time a week?* This is an astounding value of thirteen cents an hour. The decision was made. I just confirmed with my wife a few minutes ago that the plan is still working after three months.

The motive for presenting these ten principles of productivity is not to increase work volume but rather to accomplish the work that needs to be done—and to do it within the totally reasonable twelve hours of allotted time—so that you can experience the wonderful conversation and community with family and friends that God intended for you. Work is an important ball to juggle, but we must remember that it is only a rubber ball, while family, health, friends, and integrity are balls made of glass. Or, to say it another way, the goal is not to make a living but to make room for living.

|||█ My Thoughts on This Chapter █|||

❑ Below is a list of the ten principles of productivity. Ask each person to take a few minutes to rank the ten principles in order of possible effectiveness for him or her personally (1 = the most effective; 10 = the least effective, or it doesn't apply to their situation).

_____ The Principle of Goal Setting

_____ The Principle of the To-Do list

_____ The Four-Hour Principle

_____ The Principle of Giftedness

_____ The Principle of Delegation and Teamwork

_____ The Principle of Positional Identity

_____ The Principle of Commute Reduction

_____ The Principle of Results for Flexibility

_____ The Principle of Outsourcing

_____ The Principle of Efficiency

❑ Go around the room and ask each person to share their number one choice and how it could most help them if they were to apply it. Based on your available time, move to everyone's second and third choices.

❑ Share your number one discovery from this chapter.

❑ Identify and share one personal action step you will take in making more room for life.

❑ Community-Building Exercise: Divide group members into groups of two or three. Each person should pick one principle to focus on for the week and share it with the other person(s). Call each other once a day to see how things are going. Share your experiences at the next group meeting.

Personal Action Steps

CHAPTER 10

Discovering the Convivium

The Importance of Sharing a Meal

What if every member of the family completed their work Monday through Saturday between the hours of 6:00 A.M. and 6:00 P.M. What if a family, and even a collection of people living in the same neighborhood, sought to live by the principle that all work ceased after 6:00 P.M.? No housework, laundry, e-mails, reports, home projects, homework, organized sports—and no evening meetings at the church.

This has become the lifestyle of my family and a growing number of other families who want to exit the chaotic lifestyles, reclaim our lives, and connect with a circle of people God has given us. The Hebrew Day Planner laid out in chapter 5 provides a broad guide to accomplish this lifestyle. As in an exercise program, we falter and flex, but we always come back to the plan with the belief that it will replenish our souls.

From the time our family made this commitment to the time when it became the new rhythm for our life together was roughly two years. As mentioned in chapter 6, old habits die hard. Everything seems to favor the status quo, even if we know it's harming us. There were, and still are, many causes, activities, and temptations that desire to pull us back into the lifestyle that promises so much but in the end gives very little.

For our family, housework has been the easiest area to address. My wife works a part-time job outside the home that has a flexible schedule. She's laid out a schedule where she does her shopping, laundry, and errands during the 6:00 A.M. to 6:00 P.M., Monday through Saturday, time frame. She also has a very disciplined personality.

My work is another area that has finally come together. One of the driving forces for this adjustment is the fear of repeating the forty-five days of sleepless nights I experienced several years ago. Fear is sometimes a healthy motivator. Knowing that work will cease at 6:00 P.M. causes me to be more intentional and efficient with regard to how I use my day.

The third area to come under alignment was church. Gratefully, we had begun years ago to transition our church from a central campus program model to a place-based community model (see my previous book *The Connecting Church*). Deconstructing the dozens of linear circles and offering what was worthwhile to the decentralized place-based communities was a daunting task, but today we, individually and corporately, are reaping the benefits. Spiritual work is happening throughout the week; it's just happening within the neighborhood rather than at the church facilities. Last night a neighbor stopped by, with a ten-minute notice, to discuss plans for celebrating the Passover meal as a community. We discussed the action items casually in my living room for about thirty minutes and then spent another thirty minutes pondering ways God may be calling this precious lady to use her gifts and passions in the future. Some may call this a meeting, but it feels very different to me.

Without question, the most difficult area to align has been our children's activities. Children's activities are simply not family friendly. For the first time in our family's history, we have said no to spring baseball leagues. It was amazing the well-intentioned pressure we received from coaches and other parents, but we stood by our guns. The Frazee family will not be sitting outside on a school night until 10:00 P.M., watching our children play a game, knowing that they haven't finished their homework for tomorrow. Funny thing, our boys haven't said one word about it. (Chapter 12 will present practical ideas on how to deal with issues like children's sports and work.)

One of the reasons some people resist this model is that they're not sure what they'll do with the time together once it is successfully freed up. You may recall from chapter 7 that this was one of the biggest concerns for the town of Ridgewood, New Jersey, as they collectively took a night off from all activity. What would they do with each other? There are some families who don't spend thirty minutes together on a regular basis, so how could they envision four hours! This chapter lays out the new vision. It is very simple but profound in the results.

The relational season of the day (the beginning of the day for the Hebrew) lasts from 6:00 P.M. to 10:00 P.M. It is divided into two parts: 6:00 P.M. to 8:00 P.M.—the time for the meal—and 8:00 P.M. to 10:00 P.M.—open time.

The Meal

The table is the centerpiece and heart of community. This is an ancient belief—a tradition that has stood the test of time. The "making room for life" vision is an invitation to come to the table, to share a meal and conversation with a circle of family and friends each evening. When we wake up each day to face the wonderful work that is before us, whether it takes place at school, the office, the factory, the farm, or the home, we do so with a longing—a genuine passion to gather at the table at dusk to partake of a meal that sustains us and to listen to another page in the novel of the people God has graciously brought into our lives. When this event takes place, our souls send a signal to our minds that this is right. Something in us tells us that this is a major demonstration of the connection requirement we were designed to reach. It is no mistake that Jesus chose the meal as the place where the community remembers his saving work on the cross.

Some call it "the convivium." *Convivium* is the Latin word for "feast." The convivium invites us to feast on whole foods that nourish our body and to feast on the conversation of those who sit around the sacred table of community and thus to nourish our minds and souls. The proponents of the convivium are sometimes known as supporters of the "slow-food movement" for two reasons. First, the food is good for us and worth savoring. Second, and more important, this is the moment we've been looking forward to all day. It is the prize, the reward, for a day of hard work. When one's definition of success is measured in accumulation, then the meal has little value other than to be the fuel to keep us working until we have all the stuff we think we need or until it is paid off. Comedian George Carlin says that under this arrangement "a house is just a pile of stuff with a cover on it."[46] However, when one's definition of success is conversation, then the meal becomes the end, not merely the means. Discovering the convivium is at the core of trading accumulation and activity for conversation and community as a way of life. With this vision, the house becomes a place of safety, replenishment, and refuge with a cover on it. In simple terms, to miss the meal, or to rush it, can only spell failure.

This is not the experience of most people I know. We are the "Fast Food Nation." The fast-food movement emerged out of the development of the superhighway system and the suburb. In 1956, Congress passed the Interstate Highway Act under the leadership of President Dwight D. Eisenhower. He had pushed hard for such a bill because he had been enormously impressed by Adolf Hitler's

Reichsautobahn, the world's first superhighway system.[47] This new roadway system gave birth to the fast-food industry. Along these highways, fast-food restaurants popped up to serve a "liberated" people on the move. How has this changed the way we eat and live? Eric Schlosser, author of the best selling book *Fast Food Nation: The Dark Side of the All-American Meal,* provides this alarming report:

- In 1970, Americans spent about $6 billion on fast food; in 2001, they spent more than $110 billion.
- Americans now spend more money on fast food than on higher education, personal computers, computer software, or new cars. They spend more on fast food than on movies, books, magazines, newspapers, videos, and recorded music—combined.
- On any given day in the United States about one-quarter of the adult population visits a fast-food restaurant.
- An estimated one in three workers in the United States has at some point been employed by McDonald's.
- What we eat has changed more in the last forty years than in the previous forty thousand.
- The Golden Arches are now more widely recognized than the Christian cross.[48]

While some fast food is rather tasty, it is rarely good for you, and it is rarely eaten at home around the dinner table. Very few people can envision pulling out the family dishes and sitting around the dining room table with a Big Mac or a Big Beef Burrito! Fast food is made fast and eaten fast, usually in the car on the way to some activity.

If we are to make room for life, we must discover the convivium. We must return to a time when food is placed back on the table— and it is worth eating slowly—and where conversation is not rushed. There are some signs that things may be changing. First, at the time of the writing of this book, McDonald's had reported its twelfth consecutive quarter of losses. Second, there is a movement begun in Italy called "the convivium"—a growing group of people around the world who are proactive in promoting the return of the slow-food movement. There are currently sixty-three chapters of the convivium in the United States.

Food Preparation

I have the wonderful blessing of being married to an Italian woman who has worked hard to perfect her culinary skills. She was taught the basic elements of cooking from her family and has built on it to provide our family with a wide palette of healthy food. Coming to the table at the Frazee household is always a treat. One of the things we've lost with the onset of the fast-food movement is the training of the next generation of cooks. (By the way, the art of cooking doesn't have to be limited to women. In several families I know, the men are the primary chefs, and they do it quite well.)

One of the keys to a good meal is that it must be wholesome and good for the body. The meal doesn't have to be elaborate or fancy—although this is certainly encouraged. If no one in your family knows how to cook a full meal, I would encourage you to see who could pick up this important role. It can certainly be shared. If you have children, it's important to pass down this art to them so that their families will have access to the convivium in the future. If there is not a full meal placed on the table, it is less likely that people will gather around it for very long. In *The Rituals of Dinner*, Margaret Visser tells us that "the average length of an American dinner, with or without TV, is thirty minutes, which suggests that not a great deal of discussion is taking place."[49]

Consider alternatives as you learn to cook or don't have the time to cook. One option is to find a handful of simple recipes that are wholesome and good for you, and cook in large quantities and freeze the meals. There are several cookbooks that show you how to do all of your cooking in one day a month (see, for example, *Frozen Assets: How to Cook for a Day and Eat for a Month*).[50] Entire cookbooks are devoted to Crock-Pot recipes that enable you to start a meal in the morning (see, for example, *The Slow Cooker Ready and Waiting Cookbook: 160 Sumptuous Meals That Cook Themselves*).[51] Cooking Light publishes the *5 Ingredient 15 Minute Cookbook,* which includes ninety-four delicious quick-to-fix dinners for the family.[52] (FYI: my wife has stood over my shoulder for this entire paragraph.)

One of the best options, whether you are a gourmet cook or a beginner, may be to share a meal with neighbors. The workload is spread out and the conversation is expanded. You should do this at least once a week, if not twice a week. It's also great for people who are single, for single parents, and for empty nesters. When only two people are in the house there is a tendency to skip a quality meal or go out to eat regularly. I think taking the time to sit down to a meal with conversation is a better option. Whatever your approach or situation, preparing a meal for the convivium takes planning and intentionality. If you wait until the last minute, your dinner experience will almost invariably be pushed to fast food instead of slow food.

Setting the Table

After 6:00 P.M. all work is to cease. Therefore, if the table is not set by 6:00, this act is not one person's responsibility but a part of the overall festival of the meal—a family affair, in other words. If you live in a home with a kitchen table and a dining room table, I strongly recommend you have your dinners each night in the dining room. We purposely bought a table for the kitchen that only accommodates four chairs comfortably, which forces us, as a family of six, to hold dinners in our dining room. I am convinced this will be one of the strongest memories my children have after they leave the home. (Eating outside whenever possible is ideal, too. I love eating a great meal outside.)

What is set on the table should become a unique mark of each family. If your personality leans toward that of a Martha Stewart, then go all out. No matter what your bent is, though, you should seek to be creative and build traditions. For our family, we enjoy picking out unique dishes—with no particular need for everything to perfectly match. As we travel we like to pick up unique things for use at the dinner table. Each piece, whether it holds bread or pepper or vegetables, has a special place in our hearts and brings back memories each time it is used. After ten years or so, what's on your dinner table will remind your family that you have a history together—even before a single word is spoken.

On Saying Grace

I grew up in an unchurched home. When I became a Christian in 1974 at the age of fourteen, I had to make arrangements to get to church and back home by myself. The church was about a twenty-minute drive from my house. If I wanted to come back for Sunday evening worship, which I always did, it made the most sense to stay at the church all afternoon or to go home with a family that lived near the church. There was one particularly gracious Italian family that invited me to their house almost every Sunday for a great meal—usually pasta and salad. The father was a successful independent grocer who had many tales of buying and selling produce that captured my attention.

At dinnertime we would all gather around the table, and he would "say grace." This was a new experience for me. This successful man would bow his head and humbly thank God for providing the food we were about to eat. I had never heard of such a thing. It seemed to me that he had worked very hard to get to where he was and that he should take all the credit. However, he humbled himself in the presence of his family and declared his gratitude to God. There were times when everyone else's head was bowed and eyes were closed, and I'd look up and stare at him. I desperately wanted to grow up and be like him. I wanted to raise a family and demonstrate God's love and protection on our family, just as this father did.

Well, I've been married to his beautiful daughter now for over twenty years, and I see it as a great honor each night to say grace to God on behalf of my family of six. I concur with the heart of William

Shakespeare, who wrote, "O Lord, that lends me life, lend me a heart replete with thankfulness."[53] Alda Ellis, in her heartwarming book *A Table of Grace*, writes this:

> The family dinner is indeed a legacy to be passed on from one generation to the next. I believe that it is more important for our children to know who the head of the family is than who the head of the country is. So many positive things begin while seated at the dinner table—respect, good communication skills, proper table manners, the humble thanking of God for our blessings.[54]

On most nights we simply hold hands, and I offer the grace. On certain nights we will ask a member of the family to do the honors. If we have guests at the table, we always pray for God's blessings on them. If a member of our family is missing from the table, we always pray for their safe return to us. On many nights we observe Communion. We have matzo crackers in the buffet next to the dinner table. At the beginning of the meal I pass around the cracker, and everyone breaks off a piece. A member of the family then says grace but focuses the prayer on the sacrifice of Jesus on the cross—the ultimate act of grace on our behalf. At the end of the meal and conversation, I pass around a goblet of wine that sits by my place setting, and every person sitting at the table takes a drink—and so we close the meal focused on the blood of Christ. Saying grace is an absolutely essential part of the Christian convivium.

The Art of Dinner Table Conversation

The dramatist W. S. Gilbert once said, "It isn't so much what's on the table that matters as what is on the chairs."[55] Jacques Pépin, chef for Oprah Winfrey, makes this observation about the importance of family meals:

> My daughter is twenty-six years old, and when she comes home, we eat together as we always have. I know people who probably haven't had a conversation with their children for years,

because the children come home, say, "Hi, Dad," and go straight to the refrigerator for a sandwich. The dinner table should be the stage where you talk at the end of the day. The conversation may not always be pleasant—maybe you have an argument about what happened in school—but it is a very necessary thing that brings the family together.

Food, and the sharing of food, sustains human relationships more than anything else, including sex. It's an extraordinarily important part of the family structure and the common denominator that brings people together in a house—certainly in mine! Maybe it sounds corny, but for me, food is an expression of love, because you always cook for "the other"—wife, child, lovers, friends. Food is life.[56]

Conversations around the dinner table are not a new idea. In *The Rituals of Dinner,* Margaret Visser gives us this history lesson:

> Plato's great dialogue, *Symposium,* Xenophon's *Symposium,* Plutarch's *Symposiacs* and *Banquet of the Seven Sages,* Macrobius's *Saturnalia* were the ancestors of collections of *Table Talk* or *Propos de table* which have continued as a minor tradition of European *belles lettres* down the centuries. Athenaeus wrote what must be one of the longest versions on record: fifteen volumes of chat, called *The Sophists at Dinner.*[57]

Dinner-table conversation is a lost art and practice in our society. Yet it is the thing we should long for with great intensity. While there is a great deal written on how we should approach this conversation (*Rules and Orders of the Coffee House of 1674,*[58] for example), we need not make it so complicated that today's novice is overwhelmed and avoids it altogether. At its most profound and simplest level, conversation at the dinner table involves each person sharing what happened throughout that day. I believe a significant part of the connection requirement is met when we have a chance each day to share the events of our day, no matter how mundane, with a circle of family and friends who are hanging on each word we say because they genuinely care about our welfare and are interested in our story.

Here's how it works in our family. After we've said grace and the food is on each person's plate, we simply tell about our day. We start with the family member or friend sitting on my left. Each person starts with the time they got up and then chronologically unfolds the details. When we first made the decision to do this, I wasn't sure my children would cooperate. Would my teenage daughter share her day with her younger brothers, or would she be willing to listen to them share their day the way boys share? Would they really be interested in the details of Mom's and Dad's day in such a way that this was a meaningful experience for us? Would everyone get tired of it and do it only to placate my desire to have a dinner that lasted more than fifteen to thirty minutes?

I've been utterly amazed at the value of this simple experience. I remember coming home one day and asking one of my sons to tell me how his day went. He responded back, "Oh, I'm saving it for dinner tonight!" On another occasion we'd had an evening where we didn't tell about our day, and one of my sons asked the next afternoon if he could share two days at dinner since we had missed the night before. He wanted to share something from the day before that he hadn't had a chance to share.

After doing this for some time I'm convinced we were created with the need to share our days with a circle of family and friends. Such a simple thing to do, but I believe the long-term results of this kind of conversation lead to relational, physical, emotional, and spiritual health. For this experience to be successful, parents must not use this time to scold or correct a child at the table who is sharing his or her day. To do so will certainly stop the flow of information during future dinners. Adults must not do this to each other either.

One night a week we have a biblical or spiritual discussion. For these special evenings we usually invite a family from our neighborhood. Our church provides a simple study guide that can be used by a family to stimulate discussion around the same Scripture passage on which the upcoming Sunday's sermon is based.[59] The guide usually presents a thorny modern-day case study that leads to a discussion on how to apply the passage of Scripture for that week. In a recent study in the book of Exodus we had meaty discussions on a Christian who lost his job, a couple who couldn't have children, a teenager who struggled with the notion that Jesus was returning to earth, the life of Dietrich Bonhoeffer, and a prayer effort in Cali, Columbia, that brought down the infamous drug lords there. Everyone's idea is heard, and gentle disagreement is encouraged. As a matter of fact, sometimes we invite half of the table to argue against the other side. By means of these wonderful discussions, the members of my family are learning to think critically about how their faith connects with everyday life. This may be the number one legacy I leave my family—the legacy I hope they'll pass on to their children.

The meal is not over until the table is cleared and the kitchen cleaned. This ritual of cleaning does not fall to one person but to everyone who has partaken of the meal. It is a privilege and an extension of the festival. When this is completed, the mealtime is done for the day. Under normal circumstances, it will take from 6:00 P.M. to 8:00 P.M. to have a meal (from the setting of the table to the end of the cleanup). We all await the dawning of a new day with the promise of its successes and challenges, all to be shared that evening at the convivium.

Open Time

Once the meal is completed, there are still two hours until bedtime (8:00 P.M.–10:00 P.M.). Since work is not allowed, what is a person to do? Discovering what to do during this time frame each evening has been one of the most exciting changes in my life over the last five years. As a type A, hard-driving, boundaries-challenged person, I couldn't imagine not working on something. Here are the three rules to guide this final watch of the day:

- Do not do any work.
- Stay out of the car as much as possible.
- Keep the lights and noise low (God is getting you ready for a great night of sleep).

I have found the options endless:

- You can journal or have a devotional time alone.
- You can play a game as a family. We love playing a game on the floor while watching a sporting event on television.
- You can play a musical instrument. I love to go to my neighbor's house next door. He plays a folk guitar and I'm a beginner banjo player. Sometimes others join us and sing along. My oldest son has recently picked up the harmonica, which adds a nice sound to our attempts at bluegrass and country gospel music.
- You can listen to a CD with your headphones.
- You can take a walk or pop in on a neighbor for ten minutes.
- You can sit out in the front yard if the weather permits and see who stops by.
- You can play a video game or watch a little television.
- You can read a novel or a good magazine.
- You can invest some time in your hobby.
- You can dance with your spouse or child.

I don't know how you feel now that you've read this chapter. You may feel you have too many commitments and schedules to keep to ever see this become a reality in your life. Don't worry. In chapters 12 and 13 I'll make specific suggestions on how to begin making the transition. Right now all I want to know is if this is the kind of life and pace you long for? When I think of making room for life, this chapter describes what I wanted but was missing in my life. I hope it does for you as well. This is not a way of life for the financially wealthy. As a matter of fact, rich people seem to have the hardest time getting to this kind of life because they have so many options to distract them. This is the simple way of life God intended for all of us. I invite you to come to the table and take in the wonderful convivium!

My Thoughts on This Chapter

❏ Share one of your most meaningful dinners as a child or as an adult. What are the common characteristics between your experiences?

❏ How many dinners do you share with family and friends in an average week? Are you satisfied with this number? What are the causes of your success or struggle?

❏ Do you feel that sharing the convivium (or evening meal) is simply an old-fashioned idea with no real chance of success in today's busy society, or do you feel it is essential and must be rediscovered? Explain your response.

❏ Identify the one or two greatest obstacles in experiencing the convivium. Brainstorm possible solutions.

❏ The Hebrew Day Planner requires that everyone finishes their work by 6:00 P.M. (adults and children). If you eliminated all office work, schoolwork, and housework, what are the top three things you would envision doing with your free time after dinner?

❏ What do you think about the following statement?

> I believe that a significant part of the connection requirement is met when we get a chance each day to share the events of our day, no matter how mundane, with a circle of family and friends who are hanging on each word we say because they genuinely care about our welfare and are interested in our story.

Have you ever gone through a season in your life when you shared your day with someone nearly every day? Explain your experience.

❏ Share your number one discovery from this chapter.

❏ Identify and share one personal action step you will take in making more room for life.

❏ Community-Building Exercise: Divide the group into dinner-size groups (maybe two or three families at the most). Have each group share the convivium between now and your next meeting. Follow the outline for the evening presented in this chapter. Share your experiences with each other at the next meeting.

Personal Action Steps

CHAPTER 11

The First Church of the Neighborhood

Bringing Church Home

In 1990 I became the senior pastor of Pantego Bible Church in Fort Worth, Texas. My goal, with God's guidance and help, was to revitalize this struggling congregation. The counsel of experts and blue-chip practitioners at that time was to start as many programs as possible that would attract new people to the church. The logic was sound. Today's busy American shops as a consumer in places that offer the most options and the most excellence.

If you were going to be a "church on the move," you certainly needed to offer small groups along with the myriad of other quality programs. So small groups it was. I operate on the principle of "speed of the leader, speed of the team." If we were to install this mammoth, leadership-intensive ministry, every staff member needed to get in a small group in order to model correct behavior. Therefore, it became a requirement for everyone on staff—including me—to be in a small group. Each year staff members would sign a covenant that included involvement in a small group sponsored by the church. Continued employment required one's signature on a perennial document as well as participation in a church-sponsored small group.

So this meant I needed to get into a small group. In the past I had participated in and led many small groups. But we were between groups, and this was a good opportunity to form a group that really ministered to my wife and me. I thought to myself, *I'm the senior pastor of the church. I bet I can recruit a stellar small group—the Mother of all Small Groups.*

The majority of American churches establish their connections in small groups based on a contractual theory. Simply put, it works something like a pickup baseball game. The two strongest kids are the captains. The rest of the children line up, and the selection process begins. How are members selected? From the strongest to the weakest. The same dynamic happens when forming small groups. We *contract* with others to be in our small group based on an upward association and invitation. In the end, these kinds of social contracts fail and lose their sizzle because they are contrived from the beginning.

My wife and I made a list of our dream team. These were some of the best individuals I'd ever met. To form them as a team—a small group—certainly meant we were the odds-on favorite to win the Little League World Series of Small Groups. Before we had our first group meeting, no one knew each other. We started meeting one evening every other week for about two and half hours. I was fulfilling my covenant as a staff member of our church.

As this small group was forming, something else was taking place organically that I neither asked for, looked for, nor expected. At the time we lived on a street with about eighty houses on it. There were no cul-de-sacs, just a single street used by many to reach a main artery street. But the street had a certain charm. The neighborhood was developed in the early 1960s in what was once a thriving pecan orchard. We bought a small ranch house on the street. Not long after we moved in, a new neighbor moved in two doors down. Fictitiously, I'll call them Kent and Susan. Kent and Susan had two children, were unpretentious, and didn't go to church. Kent was particularly gregarious. He would often meander over to the house in the evenings or on the weekends just to hang out for a few minutes or a few hours—I don't remember. I enjoyed his company.

On many Saturdays he would take his newspaper and sit in our family room to read it. He would help himself to a cup of coffee or a cold drink from the refrigerator. Saturday morning was my lawn time. I put on some worn-out clothes and leather gloves and got after it. The first time Kent appeared on a Saturday morning, I walked into the house for a drink of water and found him sitting on my sofa reading the paper. *Oh, no!* were the unspoken words in my head. *I have to host Kent instead of getting my work done.* I sat down and said, "So, Kent, hooowwws it going?" He peered over the newspaper and said, "I'm fine. Hey, isn't Saturday morning your lawn day?" "Why, yes," I responded. "I thought so," he said. "I do my lawn on Friday afternoon and like to relax and read the paper on Saturday morning. So if it's okay with you, why don't you get your work done and I'll read the paper, and then later we can catch up." It was music to my ears. I was out of there before he could get past one frame of a comic strip.

About a half hour later I came back in the house. This time my wife was "hosting Kent." She ran into the same experience I did. As I went back outside, I thought, *How strange that he would come over to our house unannounced, help himself to whatever's in our refrigerator, and then not require us to host him. It was strange, but I liked it—I liked it a lot.* It was here that I learned my first principle of authentic community: It breaks out when you can sit in a room together and enjoy each other's presence but not feel a need to always talk.

One day Kent came to my house to borrow a ladder. I was more than happy to oblige. A few days later he brought the ladder back.

About a week later I was standing with Kent in his garage and noticed a ladder in the back corner. When I asked him why he had borrowed mine, he evaded the question. It was then that I learned my second principle of authentic community: Drawing people into a circle of friendship involves not only helping out but also reaching out. People want to know they are needed. Kent made me feel that I was being helpful to him and his family. I liked that feeling—and he knew it.

Kent and Susan introduced us to the neighbors across the street from them—a married couple with one child who was our daughter's age. They didn't go to church either. We began to hang out together, which was so easy, given that we were neighbors. Sometimes we would spend hours together. Many times our encounters only lasted for five or ten minutes as we left for work or took out the trash. Here I learned a third principle of authentic community: It happens best when we spend frequent and spontaneous time together.

Before I even knew how to define it or what to call it, these relationships expanded to others in our neighborhood and captured the hearts of our family. I distinctly remember the Friday evening when my wife and I drove down our street on our way to our church-sponsored small group hosted at a house twenty minutes away. We had hired a baby-sitter to be with our kids. We loved the people in our small group dearly, but with our busy lives we just couldn't get together outside of the every-other-week meeting. As a matter of fact, given the contractual theory of relationships, we still would have chosen them over our neighbors. But the proximity issue was starting to overcome us with wonder. As we drove down the street on a beautiful spring evening, the neighbors were out in full bloom. We waved as we went by, wishing we could stay home with our children and neighbors. That's when the lightbulb in my head turned on. What if my neighborhood families could count as my small group? My heart leaped with excitement. I shared the idea with my wife. I could tell by the look on her face, before she ever said a word, that we were of one accord.

There was, however one problem: This would not qualify as a church-sponsored small group. *"Wait a minute,"* I thought. *"I'm the senior pastor. I can declare this to be a legitimate church-sponsored group!"* And I did. Over the next couple of years my team at church worked to understand the ideas behind this model. As we did, we gave ourselves more and more to the neighborhood. Here I learned a fourth principle of authentic community: The contractual theory is not authentic, but the communitarian theory is. This theory suggests that when we give ourselves to the people around us, even though there is diversity that we may not be attracted to, authentic community has a real opportunity to be experienced and found to be very desirable.

Not long after the light came on in my head, Kent and Susan moved. I picked up the mantle and moved forward. As thirteen years on that street came to an end, my worlds had been seriously consolidated. While the neighborhood gatherings looked more like a scene out of *My Big Fat Greek Wedding* than a traditional small group meeting, at the core there was a growing spiritual depth. A number of families and singles began to attend church with us on Sundays, but not all. Some went to other churches. Many came to put their faith in Jesus Christ; some did not. The experience was intensely intergenerational—from singles to married couples, from infants to senior citizens. For the first time in my life my world of Christian fellowship merged with my world of relationships with irreligious people and seekers. It felt right—so right—to the very core of my spiritual bones. (Reread chapter 4 if you don't fully understand what I'm talking about here.)

Eighteen years later it's not only the core operating principle of my family's life—a circle of life—but it's the direction our entire church has taken. It took seven years for this to become a new part of the DNA of our church. My commitment to this transition was so strong that I bet the farm on it. While we lost a few cows and chickens along the way, it was worth it. Today our church has place-based communities (home groups) everywhere.

Lyle Schaller, a wise sociologist and popular church consultant, said several years ago that "the biggest challenge for the church at the opening of the twenty-first century is to develop a solution to the discontinuity and fragmentation of the American lifestyle."[60] I strongly believe this simple strategy goes a long way toward solving this societal ailment.

Six years ago my family moved about three miles down the road. We left our wonderful neighborhood after much prayer in the bonds of a tight-knit community. The vision for this move was to take what we had learned and move into a new neighborhood to see if we could reproduce this simple idea. This time we wanted the community to have an intentionally spiritual foundation. So we decided to begin with this focus.

We moved into a neighborhood where several families from the church already lived. Our intent as we made this move was to stay home more and consolidate what it meant to be a follower of Jesus into this new circle of ninety houses. What Kent did in the last neighborhood was now my calling. We took walks, had neighbors over for dinner, and hung out in the front yard (weather permitting) instead of the back. We determined to stay with it and to consolidate as much of life as we could into this "circle."

Shortly after we moved in we invited neighbors to a dessert get-together to explain our simple idea and ask them to consider partnering with us on "making room for life." We invited the families in the neighborhood that went to our church, families that went to other churches, and even a few families that didn't go to church at all. Would anybody show up? To our amazement, everyone we invited showed up! This was a good sign that people wanted to know their neighbors.

At our dessert time we shared our vision for the circle of life. At the core we wanted to establish the presence of a Christian community in our neighborhood. While we would have a weekly gathering called "Home Group," we would all seek to do life together in as many ways as possible. We set out our covenant of purpose with an acronym that spelled "S-E-R-V-I-C-E" (the seven functions of biblical community):

Spiritual Formation: We will help each other grow.
Evangelism: We desire for our neighbors to know Jesus Christ.
Recreation: We will have fun together.
Volunteerism: We will volunteer to help our church.
International Missions: We will help the church internationally.
Care: We will care for each other.
Extending Compassion: We will help the poor and needy in our community.[61]

We would not accomplish each of these purposes every week, but over the course of a year, we wanted to be able to point to tangible things we had done together to achieve our aim.

All the families that came to the dessert get-together were excited about the vision. All but one came on board. The family that didn't join were members at another church, and they regularly attended Sunday evening worship there—and Sunday evening was the time we had decided we would all formally gather as a group.

Over the last six years we've seen lives transformed. People have come to faith in Christ, and many have been baptized right in our neighborhood. Each year we share a plan for our personal spiritual growth through a tool called the Christian Life Profile.[62] We study the Bible together using a Bible study program developed by our church called The Scrolls.[63] We have celebrated Seder Passover meals together at Easter and studied the Bible together on a weekly basis. We have cared (**C**) for each other in so many ways—after the death of a parent, when someone was ill, when people were struggling in their marriages, or simply by collecting each other's mail when someone is out of town. Together we have volunteered (**V**) and served by adopting a large landscape bed at the church, worked together on a rotation basis in the children's ministry on Sunday morning, and work as a team at the annual October community carnival held at the church. We've ushered in the New Year together for the last six years in a row. We've taken at least a dozen vacations together. We routinely have dinner together. We participate in international missions (**I**) by supporting a full-time pastor in India, as well as by raising money for Children's Bible Clubs for Indian children. We extend compassion (**Ex**) as we serve once a quarter at the local night shelter, participate each year in a three-mile walk to raise money for the Lymphoma and Leukemia Society, and deliver at Christmastime special baskets of goodies (always accompanied by caroling and hugs) to the eight widows we've adopted from our church and our neighborhood. Every Tuesday morning the women in the neighborhood demonstrate a heart for evangelism (**Ev**) and caring (**C**) as they get together to pray for the neighbors. Every Friday afternoon the men have a set tee time at a local golf course where we can have fun (**R**) and get to know the other men in the neighborhood (**Ev**). Once a month the women host a night of Bunko for all the women in the neighborhood (**R, Ev**). After six years the list of what we've done together seems endless. The powerful thing about this decentralized approach is that our church has given birth to more than a hundred groups all over the city doing the same things. This is truly the incarnational presence of Christ in a community.

How does a Home Group work? It's really quite simple. This is the way Luke describes it in the context of the early church:

> They devoted themselves to the apostles' teaching and to the fellowship, to the breaking of bread and to prayer. Everyone was filled with awe, and many wonders and miraculous signs were done by the apostles. All the believers were together and had everything in common. Selling their possessions and goods, they gave to anyone as he had need. Every day they continued to meet together in the temple courts. They broke bread in their homes and ate together with glad and sincere hearts, praising God and

enjoying the favor of all the people. And the Lord added to their
number daily those who were being saved.

Acts 2:42–47

In the language of Acts 2, Home Group in a neighborhood
involves breaking bread, enjoying fellowship, and praying together.
Let me put it another way: Once a week someone makes a pot of
soup, and anyone from the neighborhood, including children and
senior citizens, comes and goes as they're able. During the course
of your gathering, talk, pray, and plan together about what you could
do to accomplish the seven functions of biblical community (see
page 149). Because each neighborhood is comprised of a different
collection of people, each group will choose different things to fit
the makeup of the group. Our church produces a catalog you can
check out for some ideas. Of course, we have other resources available that are great for Home Groups, such as the Christian Life
Profile assessment tool, "The Scrolls" Bible study material, and
more. Just go to www.TheConnectingChurch.com for more on
these resources. One way to move forward is to have those who may
be interested in a Home Group read *Making Room for Life*. This
will help people connect with the vision and decide if they want to
become a part of it.

A paragraph of advice is warranted here. Don't push aggressively
on these activities. Let the fellowship emerge naturally, and let each
person give his or her input. Not everyone will participate in some
of the things you choose to do. That's okay. Also, planning ahead is
key. In my experience, a family typically doesn't take a vacation
unless there's some advance planning. So it is with a neighborhood
Home Group. Finally, don't refrain from inviting unchurched people
to your Home Group or other activities. Don't hold back from praying or from discussing your growing relationship with God. I believe
there is a longing inside everyone to connect with God and with a
community. This just may be exactly what they're looking for. In our
Friday golf outings, one man brings a boom box and plays worship

music, regardless of who's there. While it may be distracting for the golfer who requires complete silence, most people enjoy it. Lest you think that everything is a 24/7 religious church experience, it's just as common for us to get tickets to a Bruce Springsteen or Eagles concert and enjoy an evening of rock and roll!

As I write this chapter, four of the neighbors involved in our church and in our Home Group have gone on an adults-only vacation. Two of the families are empty nesters with grandchildren, and the other two families have kids still at home. We took care of their kids and dogs, watched their houses, got their mail, and did whatever else needed to be done. I'm sitting in my front yard writing this chapter. Any moment now they'll be home. I can't wait to see them and catch up on the last six days. As I sit here I've talked with ten other neighbors who have either driven by or walked by. My children, who haven't been in any organized evening sports activities this spring, have been playing with the other neighborhood children for hours.

It has been my experience and personal observation that churches can complicate our already fragmented lifestyles. While it is true that the spiritual nourishment and opportunity for ministry service is much more meaningful than most other things we occupy ourselves with, it seems that there is a better and simpler way to go about it. For most people who live in the sprawl of suburbia, church is its own world—disconnected for the most part from our relationships at work, in the neighborhood, and with the schools of our children.

As I noted in chapter 1, in reality church is not just one world but also several separate worlds. If you took just the seven functions mentioned earlier (S-E-R-V-I-C-E) and created them into seven separate departments, you'd likely have a management mess on your hands. Typically, each of these different areas is managed by a different staff member or volunteer who doesn't necessarily coordinate with the others. Let's say you decide to be involved in three things because you really want to take your faith seriously. You sign up for a Bible study class that meets on Wednesday night, you sign up for the church softball league that plays on Saturday mornings, and you serve on the missions committee that meets once a month on Monday nights.

Let's say you are married and your husband joins a men's Bible study that meets on Thursday nights, and he volunteers at the church on Saturday on the landscape team. You have two children, one in elementary school and the other in high school. In addition to their Sunday activities, each one has a program on Wednesday night to attend. Without question this is a lot of activity. To make matters worse, all of you are out of the house on different nights, and so you don't spend time together as a family. But another major problem exists: most often each of these worlds is disconnected from the other. Each time you meet you're dealing with a different set of relationships.

This is not bad in and of itself. The problem lies in the fact that this level of linear activity prevents you from having the time to invest in a circle of friends, which can help you meet the connection requirement. On top of that, these seven or eight linear church worlds are disconnected from the other worlds of everyday life that you manage! It is little wonder that the average new Christian loses all contact with their non-Christian friends within two years of becoming a Christian and getting involved in a church.

There simply isn't enough time for everything and everyone. But what if we could naturally blend the world of church with everyday life? You and your family remain connected to your church, because it is important and meaningful to be involved in something bigger than one small group. Plus, the value that comes from corporate worship is virtually irreplaceable.

If you're interested in this idea, talk to your pastor about it and see what he or she thinks. Offer your family to be part of a pilot program to see if it could become a great option for others in the church who have overscheduled, busy lives. Begin your test group by reading this book and discussing it.

This is the simple vision behind "The First Church of the Neighborhood." As you ponder and pray about the changes you may want to make after reading up to this point, make sure you think carefully about this spiritual anchor of being in Christian community with others who live in close proximity to you. It's a very important piece in the puzzle of truly making room for life.

My Thoughts on This Chapter

❏ Church should be central to our experience of community. Jesus wants us to experience rich connections with him and with each other. Why is it that church can often be more of an obstacle to community than a facilitator of community?

❏ What do you think someone who says "people want relationships, not another meeting" really means?

❏ As you read the story of Kent and Susan's and Randy's neighborhood, what seemed attractive or unattractive to you? Explain.

❏ What would you think if your small group adopted the seven functions of biblical community? In what ways would this enhance your sense of connection to each other? What are the roadblocks to seeing this happen?

❏ Share your number one discovery from this chapter.

❏ Identify and share one personal action step you will take in making more room for life.

❏ Community-Building Exercise: Do a simple compassion project together as a group (examples: visit your local nursing home, serve dinner at the local mission or shelter, do some house projects for a widow in your neighborhood or in your church). Afterwards, talk about the benefits of doing this as a group.

Personal Action Steps

CHAPTER 12

Life Busters
Part 1
Dealing
with Homework
and Sports

There are many opportunities and obstacles that we face in our quest to make room for life. I hope that by now you're feeling a great attraction to the principles and stories presented. It probably makes your head hurt to think about all the changes you'd have to make to achieve your goal. No doubt there are some activities in your life that you clearly know are enhancing disconnectivity, and yet you're not sure you want to give them up. That's okay. In this chapter and the next I want to help you think through some of the most common barriers to implementing this dream. I call them "Life Busters." In this chapter we'll focus on children, and in the next we'll turn to work issues.

When you're dealing with the need for change, you need to ask yourself *what level of change you are advocating.* There are three levels to consider:

Level 1: Modest Change—an improvement of the existing system
Level 2: Substantial Change—major change of existing system
Level 3: Radical Change—scrapping the old system for a new one

Not everything that needs to be changed requires a radical approach. Sometimes you just need to make a modest adjustment. If this is all that's required for effectiveness, then you should do it. Modest change is the easiest to implement and creates the least amount of conflict and discord. However, sometimes a modest change won't even make a dent in bringing relief to a chaotic lifestyle. At times the situation requires a substantial or even radical solution. This usually takes significant courage and vision. Pioneers typically are not called pioneers because they approach life with a modest adjustment here and there. If you want to find a new way of life, and if you're like most American families, it will likely require some substantial or radical action on your part.

As we look at the following common obstacles to making room for life, you'll have to decide which level of change you're advocating. Sometimes you may only need to make a modest change. However, when it comes to some issues, you'll probably need to make a substantial or radical change in order to experience any success or relief. Place a check by the approach that makes the most sense to you.

Children's Sports

This area may equal or come in second to the automobile as the greatest obstacle to making room for life (see chapters 7 and 8). Children's sports programs are not bad in and of themselves. However, in the average suburb today, sports have taken over the evening and weekend hours and have kept the family in the car and away from dinner, conversation, and spontaneous play. Here are three options to consider:

1. ☐ **Modest Change:** *Sign up your children for sports with the children from other families in your neighborhood.* This plan gives you some options. When you are at a game, you can share it with your circle of family and friends. You can even invite neighbors who are empty nesters to enjoy a game with you. For practices, adults can take turns carpooling and sitting at practices. Our family did this for years, and it helped. But having a family of four children, the plan didn't work for us over the long haul. The modest change didn't do enough to make it effective for our family.

2. ☐ **Substantial Change:** *Limit the number of sports and activities your children get involved in each year; select activities that can be done in the early afternoon, on Saturdays, or during the day in the summer.* This proposal requires you to say no—and that is substantial. But this option limits not just the number of sports but the kind of sports. Here the parent looks for sports programs and activities that are family and evening friendly with regard to practices as well as games.

3. ☐ **Radical Change:** *Boycott organized sports until your children are in junior high or middle school.* For elementary-age children, opt for pickup games in the neighborhood or local park. By the time a child is in junior high, their coordination skills have developed well. Before that time it is debatable how much benefit in developing their skills children get from playing organized sports. Also, most schools own their own facilities, thus controlling the times of the practices or games. For the most part, coaches are teachers who desire to hold practices right after school instead of coming back in the evening. This works well for families that value dinner together and settling down in the evening hours for conversation and rest. Of course, you'll need to encourage your child to discipline themselves to get their schoolwork done during the day at school or on Saturdays in order to stay in the sport. Otherwise they'll be doing homework well into the evening hours, and your family is back to square one.

This proposal suggests that physical activities and sports are appropriate for elementary-age children but that it doesn't need to be organized by a formal organization or league to be effective. When was the last time you watched four- to six-year-olds play basketball, baseball, or soccer? If you giggle as you remember this, you'll realize that it really is a bit too much for them to handle developmentally. I'm also not quite sure if these young, highly competitive parents are ready for this high drama without embarrassing themselves on the sidelines. Type A parents should be required to take a class on sideline etiquette before their child is officially placed on a team.

I remember getting to the soccer fields early one day. I was glad to watch the game preceding my child's game without having to make an emotional investment. I watched one young dad walking up and down the sidelines and yelling at his kid. He wasn't the coach. I stood next to an older and more experienced dad by the bleachers. We gave each other that raised-eyebrow look, and he said, "This is his first kid in sports. He still thinks he's going to coach his son to be the next Pelé."

Here's an alternative: Call a bunch of kids together from the neighborhood (and maybe some of their classmates) for pickup games of flag football, basketball, baseball, kickball, volleyball, whatever. They are scheduled around the family's priorities and can prove to be as much fun as (maybe more than) organized programs. A hint: Let the teenagers help lead and coach younger kids. This is the option we've finally come to embrace. It's the only one that gets the job done. I only wish I had had the wisdom and courage to do it ten years ago. (By the way, if your parents or in-laws have given this book to you—and you have children—this chapter may be the reason you received it.)

Children's Homework

Homework is another opportunity and obstacle as we seek to make room for life. It is an opportunity because a good education is a worthy thing that will serve your children for the rest of their lives. It can also be an obstacle when a child often does homework well into the evening hours. Remember that creating boundaries in your children's sports and extracurricular activities can help solve this issue.

In reality this issue can be quite complicated because there are five major reasons homework can get out of hand: (1) The child has learning difficulties and struggles with schoolwork. (2) The child is involved in too many extracurricular activities. (3) The child is highly motivated to excel in academics and has "schoolaholic" tendencies. (4) The child is not using his or her time wisely at school. (5) The teacher is not effectively teaching.

Because of the variety of factors, the three solutions below may not be adequate for you. Feel free to develop your own ideas and choose the ones that are right for you.

1. ☐ **Modest Change:** *Give your child an incentive to get his or her work done before 6:00 P.M. and to use Saturdays to get ahead.* Most schools give a child or teenager time to complete homework while in school, but he or she often mismanages this opportunity. (This is totally human, since most adults do the same thing.) You can read chapter 9 on the ten principles of productivity and help your children apply these principles to their schoolwork. What a great mentoring opportunity for you. This, however, may not be enough. You may want to try a little incentive. Each night your child completes his or her homework before 6:00 P.M., he or she gets a treat or small allowance. Because our children are older, we give them a dollar for each day. Of course there are exceptions, such as studying for tests, working on long-term projects, and so on, and their grades must reflect that they didn't rush their work just to get the treat. This practice is not uncommon in the business world. Many contracts are established with incentives to finish the work early or on time.

Saturday is also an alternative to the evening hour. Remember, in the Hebrew Day Planner, Saturday is another possible workday—

6:00 A.M. to 6:00 P.M. If you are Jewish, or a Seventh Day Adventist, you would use Sunday instead of Saturday as your workday.

2. ☐ **Substantial Change:** *Do the best you can to have your children do their homework before 6:00 P.M. and be open to B's and C's.* Children are wired differently. Some children receive A's while doing minimal work, while others work hard and long to receive B's or C's. Some kids just can't do as well in school as others. For some children, their learning styles may not match that of the typical school's teaching methods. Remember, success in one's vocational calling is not always determined by who gets the highest grades in school. As a matter of fact, sometimes the opposite is true. Success requires a balance in foundational liberal arts education; functional competencies in one's field of study; good people skills; a network; mentors; mental, spiritual, emotional, and physical health; motivation; and God's help.

If you feel that you've taken a genuine crack at the modest level of change and it didn't produce the results you were looking for, you may want to move to the substantial change level. Several years ago one of my sons was playing on an organized baseball team. One night we got home at 10:00 P.M., only to discover that he wasn't prepared for a major test the next day on Canadian history. (I realize it may be a surprise to some of you that Texans give any time to history lessons outside of Texas and the Alamo, but we do—albeit very little [just kidding].) My wife started drilling my son on endless facts and dates pertaining to Canada. By 11:30 P.M. productivity had reached an all-time low, and emotions reached an all-time high. Having quite a bit of experience with educational theories, I gave the two a much needed break and took a look at the material. This was education at its worst—an endless list of pieces of information without a good working knowledge of the big idea. Instead of having a wonderful understanding of the beauty, culture, and meaning of Canada's people and history, it had been reduced to silly dates and unrelated, dangling facts. Instead of instilling a passion to visit Canada, I figured it would take several years of reeducation and therapy to get my son to want to vacation there of his own free will. At the end, my son had logged three hours of memorization and I said, "Enough!" All this was going into his short-term memory bank for a test. In years to come he wouldn't remember anything about Canada, let alone remember taking a class on it. We told our son to do his best, and we would all own and celebrate the results. What did he get on the test? A "C." That night at dinner my son shared these results, and we celebrated together. This was a major breakthrough for our family. A child should not be discouraged from getting A's, but under certain circumstances a lower grade may be the *smarter* option.

3. ☐ **Radical Change:** *Homeschool your children.* To some this will seem like an extreme remedy. (That's why it's called radical.) Radical changes are a scrapping of the old or more common system for a new one. The key benefit of the homeschool option as it pertains to making room for life is that it puts control back in the hands of the family. Many teachers today in public and private schools are faced with managing twenty to thirty children in a classroom, which converts much of the time that should be available for instruction to crowd management or "herding." This environment is simply inefficient.

As I researched the homeschool movement as a possible option for my children, I found four substantial benefits:

1. Most children complete their work by noon or 1:00 P.M.
2. The movement has grown to include various approaches. There are programs that require the stay-at-home mom or dad to have a teaching certificate. But there are also programs that lay out all the lessons plans, use online distant learning technology, and even offer interaction with high-caliber, certified teachers.
3. Homeschooled children seem to be well-rounded. The objection of de-socialization is a myth. Whenever I encounter a child who can hold an intelligent and

delightful conversation with adults and children of various ages, nine times out of ten the child has been home-schooled. These weren't the results I was looking for but an additional reality I've had to face.

4. Homeschoolers can get a superior education. It doesn't take a rocket scientist to look at the academic results reported in reputable magazines to know that home-schoolers on the whole are outperforming those in institutional programs.

While there are many issues to consider before embarking on this journey, it is clearly an option if the modest or substantial changes don't produce the desired results. The important thing is that you are intentional and that you take action before your children are grown-up—and it becomes too late.

Without question, America has become a nation centered around child activity—carried out, generally speaking, for the welfare of the child. I'd like to suggest, however, that the overstuffed, overplanned, harried, commuter-driven lifestyles we are ingraining into our children are harmful. While our children should have lofty goals, dreams, and ambitions, they need a healthy lifestyle and healthy community in order to be able to achieve them. That's what this chapter seeks to encourage. Decide for yourself what action your family should take, and then do it.

▌▐▌ My Thoughts on This Chapter ▌▐▌

❏ Use this family case study to help ensure that everyone understands the concept behind the levels of change:

Your family wants a pool table in the house, but you don't have room for it.

Identify a modest change, a substantial change, and a radical change. Ask each group member to vote on the option they think is the best solution to the problem.

Making Room for a Pool Table
Modest Change:
Substantial Change:
Radical Change:

❏ Look at the three recommended changes in the area of children's sports. Ask each person to vote on the one he or she thinks will work best and then to tell the group why. Different solutions can be offered.

❏ Look at the three recommended changes in the area of children's homework. Ask each person to vote on the one he or she thinks will work best and then to tell the group why. Different solutions can be offered.

❏ Share your number one discovery from this chapter.

❏ Identify and share one personal action step you will take in making more room for life.

❑ Community-Building Exercise: Schedule a time before your next meeting (or for your next meeting) when you organize a sports game for the children (kickball, basketball, table tennis, and so forth).

Personal Action Steps

CHAPTER 13

Life Busters
Part 2

Dealing with the Pressures of Work

It's been stated several times in this book, but let's say it again: *Work is a good thing.* We have been created to be workers with a purpose. God works, and he has created us to do the same. The fruit of our labor is what God has designed to provide for our most basic human needs of food, clothing, and shelter. But the benefit of work goes even beyond this. There is a form of good stress, called *eustress,* that we all need for rich and fulfilling lives.[64] Work is one of the great outlets provided by God for this experience. However, we get ourselves into all kinds of trouble when we don't place boundaries on our work. Slouching over our desks, we find ourselves praying, *Dear Lord, help me to meet this self-imposed and totally unnecessary challenge.*

Keeping Work in Balance

In this chapter I want to offer some practical suggestions on how to keep work in balance with relationships and rest. There are five different workplace scenarios in which people often struggle to keep things in check: the two-income family, the single-parent family, entrepreneurs, shift workers, and business travelers.

The Two-Income Family

In my work as a pastor, I've found that the ministry areas that excel are the ones that have full-time, motivated champions leading them. The same is true with managing a family and keeping everyone and everything in balance. If there's a full-time, motivated champion properly overseeing the homestead and family, there's a greater chance for success.

Raising a family takes time, skill, and intentional planning. Anyone who would doubt this has never done it. In many two-parent families, both the husband and wife work full-time jobs outside of the home, which pays the bills but also creates significant stress for the members of the family. If this is the situation in which you find yourself, consider the following suggestions:

1. ☐ **Modest Change:** *Be highly intentional and plan ahead.* If you sense that there's no way to eliminate or reduce the second income at this time or aren't willing to consider it, you must determine that your family is going to become highly organized and intentional. This involves, but is not limited to, having a strict schedule about who is going to be where at what time; what needs to be done at what time; when the family is going to have dinner; how the dinner is going to be prepared while everyone is at work; how family members will equally share the responsibility. If both the husband and wife are going to work full-time outside of the home, then I believe home management must be a fifty-fifty workload arrangement. Divvy up the responsibilities and hold each other accountable to get things done on time and within the boundaries so that you can have some relational time with your family and friends.

2. ☐ **Substantial Change:** *Look for flexible work.* If you're convinced that you must have the income of your spouse in order to meet the basic needs of your family, but you desire to simplify your schedule and deepen your relationships, consider looking for a job that offers you greater flexibility. Look for a job that enables you to work at home or to adjust your hours (see my treatment of this idea on page 120).

3. ☐ **Radical Change:** *Downsize to fit one income.* As long as you're not overcome with debt, it will probably take up to a year to install this option for your family. If you've accumulated much debt over the years, it may take three to five years to achieve this goal. The main requirement here is to train yourself and your family to reduce consumption, to put a ceiling on your lifestyle, and to possibly downsize your residence and purchases. More and more people are making this move and finding great freedom in doing so. They are finding that less can be more—less to pay for, less to maintain. They are also discovering that less doesn't necessarily mean less quality, just less outlay of cash overall. If you purchase or rent a smaller place that produces lower overhead in monthly payments (including property taxes and utilities), it doesn't take as much furniture and accessories to decorate it nicely. Our family has adopted the practice of "quality on a smaller scale." But there is much more to life than quality things; I've contended in this book for accessorizing your life with quality relationships. Here's a couple of questions for you to ponder: Do you want to work all day and into the evening hours to pay for a large home where you never spend any time? Or would you rather lighten your payments, and consequently your workload and stress, by renting or buying a smaller house where you can hang out with family and friends? After all, as the saying goes around our house, *You can only be in one room at a time.*

Many who read these words will feel as though the substantial and radical changes are only for people with money. Nothing could be further from the truth. It is because of a lack of money that we need to look closely at these options and give up trying to keep up with the proverbial Joneses. We have certain expenses fixed in our heads as though they are necessities and rights rather than what they are in reality—optional amenities. This kind of thinking gets us into all sorts of trouble. Consider the surprising research reported by Cornell University professor Robert Frank:

> Whereas most families in the Gilded Age had to struggle to make sure their children were adequately clothed, nourished, and sheltered, these needs are no longer at issue for all but a tiny fraction of today's families. The bottom 20 percent of earners now spend just 45 percent of their incomes on food, clothing, and shelter, down from 70 percent as recently as 1920. For most families, the current economic challenge is to acquire not the goods they need but the goods they want.[65]

The Single-Parent Family

As a pastor I've never been more concerned for a specific group in my congregation than I am for the single parent. I've been married to Rozanne now for over twenty years. We are on the same page in every area that matters. We are totally committed and full of energy, and yet it still takes everything in us to make life work. I can't imagine how a single parent pulls it off. The two responses I typically receive from single parents when I ask them how they manage are "by the grace of God," or "Pastor, we're not managing!" Recently I've been so inspired by a few (and yet a growing number of) single parents who have stepped up to the plate with a bat in their hands and are knocking it out of the park. What have they done? What they've done is the only solution I have to offer. (You can decide whether it is a modest, substantial, or radical change.)

Get deeply connected to an intergenerational circle of Christian families that live in close proximity to you, preferably within walking distance. For many of us, extended family members don't live in the same town. If they do, hopefully you can rely on them to help out. Sometimes families aren't healthy enough to make helping you less stressful than doing it on your own. You must rely on Christian community for the kind of support you need, which is one of the reasons God has called us to community. Keep in mind, though, that this is not a one-sided proposal where the Christian community always gives and the single parent always takes. It is a mutual community where we help each other make up the difference when we are short. It is the strong cord of three strands that Solomon said is not quickly broken (Ecclesiastes 4:12).

Entrepreneurs

The entrepreneur has the best of all worlds and the worst of all worlds. Entrepreneurs have it the easiest because they're in complete control of their schedule. At the same time, they have it the hardest because they're in complete control of their schedule. Because they are in control, they will have the greatest freedom to implement the principles of this book without delay or red-tape bureaucracy. However, most entrepreneurs love their work, and no one stands alongside them telling them to stop. In addition, pure entrepreneurs don't know when they might get their next paycheck, so they never slow down. So, while most entrepreneurs have complete authority to make room for life, most don't.

For the entrepreneur, I have two solutions for you to consider—one requiring a substantial change and the other a radical change. (I don't offer a modest suggestion because most of the entrepreneurs I know would never choose it—so why offer it?)

1. ☐ **Substantial Change:** *Adopt the "creation time management system."* God, the most successful entrepreneur ever, applied this system successfully. The principle is found in Genesis 1. Each day God focused on one thing, and once it was done he stopped for the day. On day four he said, "I'm going to create sun, moon, and stars today." On day five he said, "I'm going to create fish and birds today." On day six he said, "I'm going to create animals and humans." Similarly, it's a wise plan for the entrepreneur to identify a focus for each day of the week. For example, Monday could be

"New Sales Leads Day." Have a 3x5 card ready with your top sales leads to contact. Get up in the morning and get after it—1–2–3. When you're done with the calls, you're done for the day. Some days it may take two or four hours; other days it may take ten. Rarely, if ever, should you work past 6:00 P.M.

I have entrepreneurial characteristics, but I wouldn't consider myself an entrepreneur in the purest sense of the word. Yet, because I have flexibility in my job I've have found the creation time management system to work wonders for me. Here's my current work-week focus:

Monday: sermon day
Tuesday: development day
Wednesday: administration day
Thursday: staff day
Friday: day off (family budget time; recreation)
Saturday: optional day (projects around the house, occasional meeting for work, and so on)
Sunday: day off (except for preaching a couple of sermons)

Monday through Saturday I have twelve hours to complete the top priorities for that day's focus—things that only I can or should do. Once they're done, I'm done for the day. I usually include checking e-mails about three times a day (morning, lunch, and late afternoon). Some days I'm done in a few hours; many days I'm pressing hard to get everything done so I can be home by 6:00 P.M.

One thing that entrepreneurial coaches teach is that you need to have one day a week for administrative tasks. Entrepreneurs typically don't like administrative tasks, and so they tend to ignore these tasks, usually to their peril. Okay, entrepreneurs, take out a piece of paper and play around with the creation time management system.

2. ☐ **Radical Change:** *Fire yourself (in other words, get a real job).* If you can't get your "entrepreneuring" in balance and you're

stressed-out beyond typical entrepreneurial eustress, you may need to put your entrepreneurship on hold for a season. An *intrapreneur* is what I see myself as. I have entrepreneurial characteristics, but I work on a team and get a real paycheck every two weeks. There are two kinds of people for whom this may be wise advice: (1) true entrepreneurs who just can't get things going in this season of life or in the current economy—and they have a family and their life is completely out of balance, and (2) people who want to be entrepreneurs but who really aren't. Being an entrepreneur has been glorified over the last few decades, but it isn't that glorious unless you really are gifted at being one.

Shift Workers

If there are any shift workers who are still reading this book, congratulations! The strict boundaries of the Hebrew Day Planner don't work well on second or third shift. However, if you have gotten to this point, I'm assuming it's because you believe in the concepts and principles but perhaps don't know how they can work for you. Let me offer two suggestions:

1. ☐ **Substantial Change:** *Do everything recommended in this book—but do it at a different time.* If you've read the previous pages, particularly chapter 5, you know that continuously working past 6:00 P.M. can and most likely will create several long-term problems physically, emotionally, and relationally. As a matter of fact, new studies show that women who work the night shift have a 35 percent greater chance of developing certain kinds of cancers than those who work during the day.[66] However, if making a change is simply not an option, you should still seek to be intentional about relationships and rest. Take the three segments of a twenty-four-hour day (productivity, relationships, and sleep), and sit down with your family and friends and lay out a plan. When will you share a meal together? (Maybe it'll be breakfast instead of dinner.) When is the family's full day of rest if it's not Sundays? Which eight-hour block of time will be used for sleeping? While I'm not passionate

about this option, I can say that working second and third shifts with intentionality and boundaries is far better than working these shifts without intentionality and boundaries.

2. ☐ **Radical Change:** *Make a move to first shift.* I hear you muttering under your breath, *Ah, the author has a great grasp for the obvious.* Yes, it's obvious but hard to do. Some, not all, choose the second or third shift because it pays more money. I just don't think it's worth what you give up in exchange. I would rather have both spouses working than try to manage second or third shift with the rest of life. The hard reality is that usually the rest of the family never completely adjusts to the shift worker's schedule.

If you embrace the principles of this book, you need to ask yourself these questions:

- What kind of changes would we have to make in our spending habits to pull this off?
- Where can we go to get out of this work cycle?
- What kind of schooling or training do I need in order to make a change to daytime labor and still earn enough money to provide adequately for me and my family?

Most careers—nursing, retail, and so forth—have daytime options that you should consider. For the last two years my daughter wanted to earn some money. She looked at working for a clothing store. We talked about it and mutually decided that she should target specialty clothing shops that close at 6:00 P.M. Monday through Saturday and are closed on Sundays. It has worked out beautifully. I don't think any store should be open past 6:00 P.M., and they should be closed at least one full day a week. (I'm guessing, though, that many people don't agree with me, since the "blue laws" regulating Sabbath behavior have been repealed in most areas of our country.)

My father-in-law was a successful independent grocer. He knew his customers and treated them with respect and helped them out when they were a little strapped financially. They in turn were very loyal to him. The chain stores came rolling into town in the 1970s and stayed open seven days a week, twenty-four hours a day. They were obsessed with making money and didn't care about the web of relationships and community, even though their commercials tried to suggest otherwise. I don't believe that people buy more just because stores are open around the clock. I just think we expand the options of when you can shop. For years I traveled through small towns where everything shut down at 5:00 P.M. In my ignorance I used to think, *What a podunk town. I could never live here.* Wow, was I wrong! My father-in-law was wise enough to spot the trend of people going to chain stores, and he sold his store while it was still worth money. A few years after it was sold, it went out of business because it couldn't compete with the round-the-clock schedule of the chain stores.

I realize that there are some people who are genuinely called to vocations that require evening work hours. I met a lady who felt called to theater. I love theater and wish they only scheduled matinee performances, but if you feel God is calling you to theater, you may not have another option. If God calls you to work a job, he will give you the strength to do it. However, you still need to be highly intentional about achieving balance between your work, relationships, and rest. Working evening hours may take its toll on your body over time, but if you believe this is what God wants you to do, then go for it.

I also want to be sensitive to the person who is genuinely stuck in a situation in which there are no apparent alternatives. These are not people who are making boat payments or wasting money on cartons of cigarettes. These are people who are ensnared in a vicious Catch-22 cycle. I'm thinking of the single parent who has a full-time job during the day and then waits tables at night to pay for medical bills and to put food on the table. She will not be able to get out of this downward spiral by herself. As I've said before, this is a clarion call to action for the Christian church—a call to come alongside and connect and restore what "the locusts have eaten" (Joel 2:25). The church must connect this person to the kind of healthy Christian community that can help in a variety of ways—from coming to be with the children, to making a place available to live in at a reduced rent, to providing financial support so she can go back to school and then secure a job that pays a better wage.

Business Travelers

The final life buster I want to address is the issue of business travel. Many people in our congregation get on a plane on Monday morning and don't come home until Friday night—and they do this week in and week out! While this can work for a time for a young single person, over the long haul it eliminates all room for living. As I write this chapter, I'm on an airplane 33,000 feet in the air, somewhere between Texas and California. I'm not suggesting that business travel is completely out of the question, but it has gotten out of hand for many people today. Consider these options:

1. ☐ **Modest Change:** *Make trips as short as possible.* When I schedule a speaking trip (on the average I do this about once a month), I look for two things: (1) Can I do it in one day, or no more than one night away from home, and (2) can I take my family along? I've found that if I lay down this goal up front, I can usually pull it off. However, when it's not a goal on the front end when the trip is being planned, you're often at the whim of others who don't necessarily take great care in navigating your personal life and health. Sometimes, when I simply must go, I sit down with my family ahead of time, and we make some intentional decisions to make up the time before I go on the trip. Sometimes I turn the trip down. I say no.

2. ☐ **Substantial Change:** *Utilize technology to minimize travel.* With the rise of some amazing technology and gadgets, it often seems that there's a better way to get things done than getting on an airplane and doing business in person. It's true that not all significant business relationships can be tended to with e-mails and cell phones, but couldn't we at least cut it in half?

A few years ago I participated in a satellite conference hosted by a popular writer and researcher. The broadcast had over ten thousand real-time viewers from all over North America. They could call or e-mail us, and we could interact with them. After the broadcast the host told me that he had talked with more people that single day than he would in smaller conferences in person over an eighteen-month period. With the rising cost of airline tickets and the aftermath of 9/11, I have to believe that video conferencing is becoming an efficient and effective option for most businesses.

3. ☐ **Radical Change:** *Switch jobs.* Many people take jobs that require excessive travel because these jobs may pay more money. But I think the cost is too high. Recently, I talked to a young married man with two small children who changed jobs to reduce travel, and he took a 40 percent cut in pay to do it. His comment on why he did this was insightful. He said, "My goal for taking the job [requiring travel] in the first place was to earn more money and improve the quality of life for my family. This was an oxymoron. I was making more money and spending all of it, but it was drastically reducing the quality of my family time. I want to be around to see my family grow up, not just fund the family enterprise. I want to be in the pictures with my wife and kids—right in the middle. I want to be with my family and friends more, so I pulled the trigger and made the change—with no regrets!"

There's so much more that could be said about work. I offer these thoughts on what I believe to be the top five life busters in the workplace. If your greatest struggle wasn't addressed, grab some trusted, well-respected friends and brainstorm on your own the modest, substantial, and radical options with regard to your particular struggle.

Let me encourage you (*encourage* means "to put courage into"). If your work is currently out of balance and squeezing living out of your life, a way to make a change to enhance your experience is very likely somewhere on the horizon. The apostle Paul advises his readers, "Were you a slave when you were called? Don't let it trouble you—although if you can gain your freedom, do so" (1 Corinthians 7:21). Throughout human history most people found their options to be few. The Bible encourages us to be content in all circumstances (1 Timothy 6:6; Hebrews 13:5; see Philippians 4:11–12). However, we live in a unique time in history where numerous options are possible. While many have used these options to create greater disorder and imbalance, you can take the options and use them to make room for life.

My Thoughts on This Chapter

Small Group Discussion

❏ Discuss how your work situation compares with or differs from that of your parents. In what ways is it better? In what ways is it worse?

❏ Ask each person in the group to pick one or two categories that best describe his or her family's work situation.

_____ one income, stay-at-home parent

_____ the two-income family

_____ the single-parent family

_____ the entrepreneur

_____ shift worker

_____ business traveler

Then take one category at a time to discuss. Follow the steps outlined below. After you've completed one category, repeat steps a, b, and c with the next category until you complete the list. (You don't have to cover a topic if no one in your group has selected it.)

a. Have those who have selected that category share the struggle they have in keeping everything balanced. (Stay-at-home parents—you're included as well. Even though you're not employed outside the home, it's possible for you to rarely be home but constantly on the run.)

b. Discuss the solutions offered in the chapter. Create new suggestions that could work better.

c. Stop and pray for the people who've shared their situations. Pray that God would give them wisdom and strength.

❏ Share your number one discovery from this chapter.

❏ Identify and share one personal action step you will take in making more room for life.

❏ Community-Building Exercise: Divide group members into groups of two or three. Each person should pick one principle to focus on for the week and share it with the other person(s). Call each other once a day to see how things are going. Share your experiences at the next group meeting.

||▮ **Personal Action Steps**

Afterword:
You Can Do It!

Making room for life" ultimately leads to a simpler life. However, the journey to get there may seem too complicated. This is precisely how I felt. This has been a ten-year journey for me, but I haven't regretted a single ounce of the work it's taken to arrive where I am today.

The goal of a mentor is to take what he or she has learned and pass it on to the receptive student early enough in life that he or she has the potential to exceed the accomplishments of the mentor. If a mentor achieves this, he or she has been successful. This is my goal. If you are young and you implement the principles of this book now, I'm convinced you'll get there faster and go further than I have. My grander goal is that you will mentor the generation coming up behind you in the principles of making room for life. If this happens and things begin to spread, our grandchildren and great grandchildren could experience a very different world.

One of my greatest joys has been to progressively introduce my four children to this way of life. While the choices they make in the future will be the final determining factor, I think they will boldly take this with them and even pass it on to others. Because they've grown up with this pattern of biblical community active in their lives, it seems to feel more natural to them. They do community gracefully.

If you are an adult under the age of sixty, there is a good chance this represents a major shift in lifestyle that may seem awkward and difficult. It is. But I'm here to tell you: YOU CAN DO IT!

Some of you have a personality that likes change and prefers "cold turkey" approaches. Go for it. Life on earth is short. Most people, though, like to put their toes in the water before they jump in. They prefer taking baby steps to help them gain confidence and courage. That's okay, too. Take the collection of ideas you've jotted down at the end of each chapter and pick one thing you plan to do differently. If you're like me, you'll find that an experience of success will encourage you to come back to your list of ideas and try another action item. If you have trouble deciding, how about just inviting one family from your neighborhood for a pot of soup, or how about taking out your lawn chairs, sitting in your front yard with a pitcher of lemonade and some extra glasses, and seeing what happens? After a while, you will gain momentum and confidence, and before you know it, you will be there. Where is there? It's a place where there is time for the most important things in life—a place where you rediscover the joys of your family and develop deep friendships with your neighbors. It's a place where you experience the richness of living life in biblical community with God and the members of his family. In other words, it's a place where there is room for life!

My Thoughts on This Afterword

Small Group Discussion

Congratulations! Your group made it to the end of the book—and, I hope, to the beginning of making room for life.

❑ Ask each group member to share the highlights of reading the book together.

❑ Identify one person in the group who has most inspired you.

❑ At the end of this afterword, each person is asked to identify an action step he or she is going to make as a result of reading this book. Share your action step with each other.

 Personal Action Steps

The first action step I will take to make room for life is:

Appendix: A Word to Church Leaders

In 2001, I wrote a book called *The Connecting Church: Beyond Small Groups to Authentic Community*. My vision for that book was for the church to become the community that Christ intended. The response has been, and continues to be, overwhelming, and it has been my great privilege to develop relationships with other leaders around the world who have been thinking along similar lines and doing something about it. Without question there is a new tribe of pastoral leaders who feel God's call on their lives to facilitate a movement toward authentic biblical community for the people who have been put under their care.

The key for the twenty-first-century church will not be in buildings, programs, or great sermons or worship services, and not even in small groups as we have known them. Church leaders must address the severe fragmentation and discontinuity of the American lifestyle as they design future plans to meet the needs of our congregations. No longer can we add an isolated program, even with grade A quality, to address one aspect of the Christian life. While we may have good intentions for doing such a thing, it may only make matters worse for the already harried and worn-out parishioner. Our thinking must be more holistic. The church's relevance and growth will largely depend on her ability to authentically "connect" people to the experience of doing life deeply together.

This new community cannot be the typical isolated small group of Christians. Rather, it must intersect the local group of citizens living in close proximity to them as well—including those who do not believe in or live for Jesus. We must see our private spaces— our homes—as centers for simple hospitality. We must stay home more; we must hang out in the front yard, not in the backyard. We must spend less time in our cars and more time with people.

The power of the gospel is found in the relationships we have with each other as Jesus has his way in each of us. People today are longing for relationships, not for meetings. We must not confuse the two. We need to lavish on others the virtue of Christ growing in us. As Francis Schaeffer has wisely stated, the Christian community is "the final apologetic."[67] In other words, the acceptance of the truth and power of Jesus Christ will fall to the authenticity of his representative community on earth.

I've been asked on numerous occasions to identify the most difficult challenge to installing authentic community in places riddled with individualism, isolation, and consumerism. Believe me, there are many obstacles, but the greatest barrier is undeniable: it's *ourselves*. It is exceedingly difficult to build functional communities on the cracked foundation of dysfunctional families and dysfunctional lifestyles. In short, you can't have a *connecting church* without *connecting lives*. As a pastor and church leader you've undoubtedly been frustrated, as I have, in trying to move your congregation toward the kind of community described in Acts 2. *The Connecting Church* was written to help church leaders design an infrastructure that facilitates authentic community in the postmodern church. *Making Room for Life* is written for your people— to help them adopt a vision for a connecting life. If we are to become the people God intended us to be, we must make room to actually experience it. This book gives my take on how to achieve this divine vision for the members of your congregation and community—and for yourself.

A good place to begin in moving your congregation in this direction is to encourage small groups of people to read *Making Room for Life* and discuss it as a group. Each chapter contains questions and comments to stimulate conversation. This should help church members see the need and benefits, and thus make your job more effective. If you've been in pastoral ministry for any length of time, you know that getting your people to see the need and benefits is one of your toughest assignments. To move forward without their awareness of their hunger is drudgery—maybe a bit like pulling teeth.

I'm not the only pastor who is thinking about these things. A growing number of church leaders are rallying around this movement. Some have been thinking about and practicing these principles much longer than I have. In addition to being a fellow practitioner, I've also been given the good fortune of being one of the secretaries or scribes who write down what many are beginning to experience in this vintage but new wineskin of community. If you are interested, we would love to have you join the conversation. Visit www.TheConnectingChurch.com to check us out.

Howard Hendricks, my beloved professor in seminary, suggested that pastors should not focus their ministry on teaching people how to do church but on how to do life. Professor Hendricks, I turn in this paper sixteen years after graduation as my humble attempt to know and do what you've talked about for so long. While it would be great to get an A, my greatest hope is that people who read it will move closer to living the life that Jesus Christ envisioned for them when he died on the cross—that many would end up leaving the chaotic life behind and experiencing the delights of connected relationships.

Notes

1. Sally Weale, "Do you often feel ill on holiday . . . but never when you're at work? If so, you could be a victim of 'leisure sickness,'" *The Guardian* (26 November 2002); read the article on the Web at www.travel.guardian.co.uk/news/story/0,7445,847874,00.html.
2. Robert Putnam, *Bowling Alone* (New York: Simon & Schuster, 2000).
3. Heard on KRLD News Radio (AM 1080) in Dallas/Fort Worth, Texas, 2002.
4. Robert Putnam, "Surprising Facts" (see www.bowlingalone.com).
5. George Gallup Jr., in Randy Frazee, *The Connecting Church* (Grand Rapids: Zondervan, 2001), 15.
6. See John L. Locke, *The De-Voicing of Society: Why We Don't Talk to Each Other Anymore* (New York: Simon & Schuster, 1998), 202–3.
7. Rich Sones, Ph.D. and Bill Sones, "Strange but True: Selling the 'me' versus 'we,'" in "Star Time" insert, *Fort Worth Star Telegram* (9 May 2003), 69.
8. See John Allen, "Ubuntu: An African Challenge to Individuality and Consumerism," *Trinity News* (posted 24 April 2002); on the Web at www.trinity/wallstreet.org/news/article_62.shtml.
9. Cited in J. Y. Mokgoro, "Ubuntu and the Law in South Africa," paper delivered at the first Colloquium *Constitution and Law* held at Potchefstroom (31 October 1997); available on the Web at www.puk.ac.za/lawper/1998-1/mokgoro-ubuntu.html.
10. Paul J. Rosch, M.D., "Social Support: The Supreme Stress Stopper," *Health and Stress: The Newsletter of The American Institute of Stress* (Issue #10, 1997), 1.
11. Ibid., 2.
12. Ibid.
13. Ibid., 4.
14. Ibid.
15. Ibid.
16. Ibid., 5.

17. Ibid.

18. Ibid., 1.

19. Paul J. Rosch, M.D., "The Health Benefits of Friendship," found in "Stress Reduction Effects of Social Support" informational packet (American Institute of Stress), 11.

20. Randy Frazee, *The Connecting Church* (Grand Rapids: Zondervan, 2001).

21. Rosch, "The Health Benefits of Friendship," 10.

22. Will Miller with Glenn Sparks, *Refrigerator Rights* (New York: Penguin Putnam, 2002).

23. John Shaughnessy, "Lack close friends? Refrigerator is clue, book says," (Louisville, Kentucky) *Courier-Journal* (2 December 2002); on the Web at www.courier-journal.com/features/2002/12/20021202friends.html.

24. See Shaughnessy, "Lack close friends?"

25. *The Andy Griffith Show* (1960–68) featured widower Andy Taylor, who divided his time between raising his young son, Opie, and his job as sheriff (and Justice of the Peace) of the sleepy North Carolina town, Mayberry.

26. Jacqueline Olds, M.D., "The Healing Power of Friendship," *Bottom Line/Health* vol. 11, no. 8 (August 1997), found in "Stress Reduction Effects of Social Support" informational packet (American Institute of Stress).

27. "The Proximity Effect," *The Vineyard Magazine* (September 2002), 14; on the Web at www.cincyvineyard.com/pdf/magfall02.pdf.

28. Ibid.

29. Archibald D. Hart, *The Anxiety Cure* (Nashville: W Publishing, 1999), 100.

30. Peter Drucker, "The Next Society," *The Economist* (1 November 2001), 4.

31. Ibid.

32. *The Legend of Bagger Vance*, written by Jeremy Leven (based on a novel by Steven Pressfield), directed by Robert Redford (DreamWorks, 2000).

33. Hart, *The Anxiety Cure*, vi.

34. Paul J. Rosch, M.D., "Social Support and Type A Behavior," in *Health and Stress: The Newsletter of The American Institute of Stress* (Issue #10, 1997), 6.

35. Hart, *The Anxiety Cure*, 193.

36. Ibid., 197–99.

37. Ibid., vi.

38. Francis Bacon, "Of Innovations," in *The Essays* (New York: Viking, 1986), 132.

39. Rick Hampson, "Are they relaxed yet? Jersey town to find out tonight—Harried citizens take a night off," *USA Today* (26 March 2002), 1A.

40. Cited in Neal Kunde, "The Lost Art of Play," *GIGGLE Parents Guide* (2002); on the Web at www.gigglemagazine.com/g-lstply.htm.

41. See "'Hockey Dad' gets 6 to 10 years for fatal beating"; on the Web at www.cnn.com/2002/LAW/01/25/hockey.death.verdict/.

42. Paul J. Rosch, "Stress and Children," *The Newsletter of The American Institute of Stress* (Issue #7, 1992), 2.

43. Valerie Latona, "Kids and Stress," *Healthy Kids* (February/March 1998), 22.

44. Cited in Ellen Parlapiano, "Simplifying Your Child's Life," *Healthy Kids* (February/March 1998), 24.

45. James Patterson, *Suzanne's Diary for Nicholas* (New York: Warner, 2001), 20.

46. George Carlin, *Brain Droppings* (New York: Hyperion, 1997), 36.

47. Noted in Eric Schlosser, *Fast Food Nation* (New York: Perennial, 2002), 22.

48. Schlosser, *Fast Food Nation*, 3–4, 7–8.

49. Margaret Visser, *The Rituals of Dinner* (New York: Grove Weidenfeld, 1991), 266.

50. Deborah Taylor-Hough, *Frozen Assets* (Milwaukee, Wis.: Champion, 1998).

51. Rick Rodgers, *The Slow Cooker Ready and Waiting Cookbook: 160 Sumptuous Meals That Cook Themselves* (New York: William Morrow, 1998).

52. Anne Chappell Cain, ed., *Cooking Light 5 Ingredient 15 Minute Cookbook* (Birmingham, Ala.: Oxmoor House, 1998).

53. William Shakespeare, *Henry VI*, Part II, Act I, Scene 1.

54. Alda Ellis, *A Table of Grace* (Eugene, Ore.: Harvest House, 2001), 15.

55. Cited in Visser, *The Rituals of Dinner*, 262.

56. Jacques Pépin, *Good Life Cooking: Light Classics from Today's Gourmet* (San Francisco: Bay Books, 1992), ix.

57. Visser, *The Rituals of Dinner*, 263.

58. "Rules and Orders of the Coffee House," in *A Brief Description of the Excellent Vertues of that Sober and wholesome Drink, called Coffee, and Its Incomparable Effects in Preventing or Curing Most Diseases incident to Humane Bodies* (London: Paul Greenwood, 1674).

59. For more information on this study tool called "The Scrolls," go to www.pantego.org.

60. From a speech given by Lyle Schaller at a Leadership Network Conference in Ontario, California, October 1998.

61. See Frazee, *The Connecting Church*, 82–83.

62. For more information on or to order the Christian Life Profile, go to www.pantego.org or to www.zondervan.com.

63. For more information on "The Scrolls," go to www.pantego.org.

64. See Hart, *The Anxiety Cure*, 21.

65. Robert H. Frank, *Luxury Fever: Why Money Fails to Satisfy In an Era of Excess* (New York: Free Press, 1999), 15.

66. See Rita Rubin, "Night shift not kind to melatonin," *USA Today* (3 June 2003); on the Web at www.usatoday.com/news/health/2003-06-03-night-usat_x.htm.

67. Francis Schaeffer, *The Mark of a Christian* (Downers Grove, Ill.: InterVarsity Press, 1970), 14–15.

The Connecting Church
Beyond Small Groups to Authentic Community

Randy Frazee

Forewords by Larry Crabb,
George Gallup Jr., and Dallas Willard

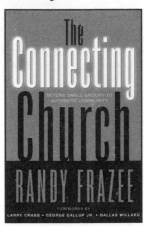

"By far the best corporate plan for spiritual formation and growth that I know of in a contemporary setting." —Dallas Willard

The development of meaningful relationships, where every member carries a significant sense of belonging, is central to what it means to be the church. So, then, why do many Christians feel disappointed and disillusioned with their efforts to experience authentic community? Despite the best efforts of pastors, small group leaders, and faithful laypersons, church too often is a place of loneliness rather than connection.

Church can be so much better, so intimate and alive. *The Connecting Church* tells you how. The answer may seem radical today, but it was a central component of life in the early church. First-century Christians knew what it meant to live in vital community with one another, relating with a depth and commitment that made "the body of Christ" a perfect metaphor for the church. What would it take to reclaim that kind of love, joy, support, and dynamic spiritual growth? Read this book and find out.

Hardcover: 0-310-23308-9

Pick up a copy today at your favorite bookstore!

ZONDERVAN™

GRAND RAPIDS, MICHIGAN 49530 USA

WWW.ZONDERVAN.COM

WILLOW
Willow Creek Resources